Evangelism...

The Unfinished Task

Robert J. Strand

GOSPEL PUBLISHING HOUSE
SPRINGFIELD, MISSOURI

02-0513

EVANGELISM . . . THE UNFINISHED TASK

This is a Workers Training Division textbook. Credit for its study will be issued
under Classification 1, Sunday School Department, Assemblies of God.

Library of Congress Catalog Card Number 81-80303
International Standard Book Number 0-88243-513-2
Printed in the United States of America

Foreword

Without apology, this book is a plea for the Church as well as the individual to become involved in soul winning. It is the unfinished commission given to us by Christ. We cannot justify our existence as a church unless we are a soul-winning, evangelizing, outreaching, loving body of believers. Could it be that we have become so sophisticated we have outgrown soul winning?

It's so easy to be sidetracked from the priorities we've set in the past. But we must return to a fervency of witness, to our very reason for being. This is a call for action.

Evangelism is something we have given lip service to in the past, but we are lax in involving every believer. We live in the day of the specialist, and evangelism has often been relegated to the "specialists" in our churches; forgetting it is an imperative for every believer. No one in the body of Christ can ignore the call for action!

I pray this book will send us to our knees in confession and then out into the highways and byways of this world to get on with the task facing us. If we don't do it, it will not get done!

You will agree with me when I say the harvest may not last much longer. What is to be done must be done very quickly!

As a boy, I worked as a harvest hand during the threshing season. When the oats, wheat, or barley had ripened, there was an urgency to cut, shock, and thresh it before a storm could come and destroy the harvest. Clouds darkening the sky were a spur to hurry and get it over with. Every person became involved. Neighbors worked together, farmers' wives cooked feverishly to feed the hungry crews, little ones helped carry water to thirsty men, and the crew was controlled by the man who ran the threshing rig—all had a job. Younger teens drove the teams of horses or tractors and the men pitched the bundles.

And what satisfaction to have completed the harvest before the rain came! I remember more than once heading for home, the harvest of a field finished just before the rain. What joy to know the job had been completed! What camaraderie in the cooperation of the harvest! It was fun and satisfying to all.

Evangelism is something we've talked about, studied, and given mental assent to, then we have pushed it aside. It must become action! It is not enough to know; we must act! This book hasn't been written to merely increase the knowledge on the subject, but rather as a prod to move all of us to the action required. Good reading, enlightening study, and positive action to you!

Contents

Contents

1

The Basic Premise

Without a doubt, the Church is the most exciting, far-reaching organism in today's world! And the Church should be the envy of every multinational company. There are more "retail outlets" where you can get the product called "the gospel" than where you can get a Big Mac, a Datsun, or a pair of Levi's!

Jesus stated with absolute certainty: "I will build my church, and the gates of Hades will not overcome it" (Matthew 16:18, *New International Version*). That is as true today as when He said it. This world system has tried its best to eliminate the Founder of the Church as well as the Church itself. But, my friend, as the songwriter has said, "The Church is alive and well!"

World events are racing toward a conclusion, and there is a frenzy of activity. Conditions are deteriorating wherever you look. It's as though we're on a toboggan ride, trying to enjoy one last fling before the party is over. Our world lives by a futile philosophy: "Eat, drink and be merry . . . "—get what you can and forget about the future—". . . for tomorrow we die."

The entire world system is built on the illusion that that which can be seen, touched, tasted, smelled, and heard is eternal and lasting. So there is a mad rush to exchange fame, fortune, and a good time for an eternity that seems distant and uncertain. But Jesus asked: "What can a man give in exchange for his soul?" (Mark 8:37, *NIV*).

This world is falling apart. Have you checked your newspaper today? It seems as though there is an attack on the very foundations of our society. Demonstrations, acts of terrorism, and rebellion are epidemic. Mankind are like a restless sea, constantly churning, seeking satisfaction and self-gratification.

A young man walked into his pastor's office and asked despondently, "Sir, can you give me one solid reason why I should keep living?" This world isn't getting any better.

Because of increased communication, we are aware that others face greater difficulties than we—famine, genocide, revolution, ever-expanding terrorism. And most of them must face these tragedies without the assurance of a personal faith in Jesus Christ.

As believers in Jesus Christ, we cannot turn a cold shoulder to the world for which He died. This is the focus of our study: what can we, as believers, do for our world? We are grieved by the overwhelming needs of mankind. It seems the problems are endless and are compounded by the magnitude of the task. How can we really make an impact on today's world of 4 billion people, the vast majority of whom are not Christian?

Have you ever driven through a large metropolitan area and observed the look of helplessness on the faces of the masses? Each of those people, blurred because of the huge numbers, is a living soul who must someday face the eternal Judge. People come in all sizes, shapes, and colors, but each one has a hurt! Each is looking for an answer to life; something to fill that "God-shaped vacuum" that's inside every human being. To some people it's just an undefinable, gnawing need.

How can we as a church minister to this world? How can we meet the desperate needs of the human soul? How can you as an individual effectively communicate God's message of hope?

The Command Is Still Valid

The Great Commission given to us by Jesus is still valid. "All authority in heaven and on earth has been given to me. Go therefore and make disciples of all nations, baptizing them . . ., teaching them to observe all that I have commanded you. . . ." But notice the Lord's promise to us: " . . . and lo, I am with you always, to the close of the age" (Matthew 28:18-20, RSV).

God's plan remains the same. In the past He called people to be His disciples and to make disciples, and this calling is still ours! His goals have not changed!

God's plan grows out of His character. He is love. He cares

about fallen sinful man. He cares far more for the needs of humanity than we do. He is God and He is sovereign. He is and always will be in control of history. He has a plan and He will triumph. And, as born-again Christians, we are part of that plan; therefore, we too will share in that great and final victory! After all, we've read the last page of the Book, and we already know the outcome!

Growth Strategy

Our strategy for growth is what can be called "spiritual multiplication." One person becomes a committed disciple. Then he reaches out to another person who also becomes a disciple, and he, in turn, reaches out to someone else who needs to find Christ. This dynamic reproduction is the essence of our outreach ministry. Evangelism has been defined as "one beggar who has found bread telling another beggar where to find bread."

When it comes to producing quality disciples, people who can serve and minister effectively as members within Christ's church, we discover there are no shortcuts! The apostle Paul indicates that this must be a process: "As ye have therefore received Christ Jesus the Lord, so walk ye in him: rooted and built up in him, and stablished in the faith, as ye have been taught" (Colossians 2:6, 7).

Compare such words as *walk, rooted, built,* and *stablished* found in this passage. You will note that each of these terms describes a *process* that involves a period of time. "Rome wasn't built in a day," and neither is the life-style of a disciple.

We live in the age of the "instant"—instant coffee, instant tea, instant hot chocolate, and instant dry cleaning. But there is no shortcut to spiritual maturity and to becoming "full-grown in the Lord" (Ephesians 4:13, *The Living Bible).* Ministry and service in the body of Christ must grow out of a relationship. Ask yourself: "Is my life a good advertisement for Christ and His gospel?" How much success would a mouthwash salesman have if he had bad breath? Would a bald-headed man be successful in selling a hair restorer? Could a very fat person entice someone to follow his diet?

The Master Pattern

A man in India told a group of missionaries: "Do you want to win Indians for Christ? The answer is simple. Fashion your lives after Christ your leader and let all see His life and power in you. Then the people of India will flock to you."

To be like Christ is to be holy. To be holy, in one sense, means keeping yourself in great spiritual shape. The apostle Paul puts it like this: "Take time and trouble to keep yourself spiritually fit" (1 Timothy 4:7, *Phillips*).

Spiritual fitness and preparation to reach our world guarantee a life of blessing and usefulness to the Lord and to needy people.

You cannot go wrong being like Christ! Jesus Christ is not superficial or weak. If He were on the earth in the flesh today, He would soon become the center of attention! Jesus draws people to Him. While He lived among men, those with hungry, searching hearts came in huge numbers because He reflected what they wanted to be like deep down inside. His life created a greater awareness of their own needs. Out of our association with Jesus, our lives should radiate this exciting difference that will attract the world to us. Our life-style should make them hunger and thirst after the life of Christ that is seen in each Christian.

Jesus challenged His followers with the pronouncement: "You are the salt of the earth" (Matthew 5:13, *NIV*). One of the ministries of "salt" is to make others thirsty—thirsty for the water of life that satisfies.

> As far as God is concerned there is a sweet, wholesome fragrance in our lives. It is the fragrance of Christ within us, an aroma to both the saved and unsaved all around us (2 Corinthians 2:15, *The Living Bible*).

Just as the pleasing, mouth-watering aroma of a cooking rib roast whets the appetite, so the fragrance of the saving life of Christ in us should whet the appetites of those around us to become sons and daughters of the living God!

Becoming Disciples

We have identified our mission and purpose, and now we

will focus on one of the weakest links in the local church. It is the lack of systematic training to prepare lay leaders to carry out this commission into the highways and byways of the world. Paul explains the order God intended in his letter to the church at Ephesus:

> And he gave some, apostles; and some, prophets; and some, evangelists; and some, pastors and teachers; for the perfecting of the saints, for the work of the ministry, for the edifying of the body of Christ (Ephesians 4:11, 12).

God's purpose in giving these gifted people to the Church is to prepare "the saints for the work of the ministry."

It is imperative that the local church integrate well-rounded discipleship training into its total program, so that, year after year, lay leaders will be raised up to be the "cutting edge" of evangelism. Through this discipleship training, lay people may cultivate a more consistent walk with God, expand their ability to minister to others, and develop their gifts for ministry. This training, coupled with actual experience and a Christlike life-style, will produce the kind of Christian who can change the world!

Often we fuss, fret, and strain, trying to implement some artificial witnessing program, and we become frustrated because the results we desire just don't happen. Some churches promote a particular plan, then lay a guilt trip on people to try to coerce them to participate in the program. But this kind of effort often results in another failure, and more guilt is heaped on the congregation because they are not "witnessing."

Jesus didn't run a school offering "three easy lessons on how to be an effective witness." He modeled a life-style for His followers and told them this kind of life could be theirs. As they lived this life, they became productive in reaching others for Jesus Christ.

Suppose you planted an apple tree in your backyard. Would you run outside every morning and say to the tree: "Tree, you are an apple tree. As an apple tree you will produce apples when you grow up. You will bear buds, which will turn into blossoms. Then you will develop tiny apples that will grow into large, ripe apples. These beautiful apples will be juicy and crunch when I eat them."

No, of course, you wouldn't do such a thing! If an apple tree receives the right amount of moisture and sunshine and the proper nutrients, it will, in due season, naturally produce apples.

Likewise, each Christian should produce the fruits of a Christian life. The real mark of spiritual maturity is when the life of Christ is evident in a person. Someone has counted the commands in the Bible pertaining to "doing" and compared them with those concerning "being." There are 27 commands to "be" for every command to "do." We tend to get so busy *doing* that we forget to *be.*

The Basic Foundational Premise

Before we can "do," we must "be." If we look carefully through the Bible, we will find God always *prepared* His servants before sending them out to minister for Him. Abraham, Moses, Jacob, Daniel, David, and Jesus are a few examples. Preparation always comes before ministry, and then continues during ministry. Everyone that God has used in dramatic, wonderful, exciting, and not so exciting ways, first went through the process of "becoming."

For example, take a look at Moses. During his first 40 years of life he learned to be a "somebody"—he was "the son of Pharaoh's daughter" (Hebrews 11:24). During the next 40 years he became a "nobody"—he became so humble that he needed a mouthpiece to speak for him. Then, during the last 40 years of his life, he became an "anybody"—"Moses was the humblest man on earth" (Numbers 12:3, *The Living Bible*). There we have 80 years of preparation for 40 years of ministry!

But we are action people! We feel the compulsion to act; we just have to be doing something! We tend to equate action with spirituality. We often think the people who are the busiest are the most spiritual. Like Elijah, we must learn that God may not be in the storm or the noise or the wind, but in a "still small voice." Becoming before doing is contrary to our natures; we would rather do and then become. But God has a better plan— *become* and then *do!*

When we become what God wants us to be, we can minister for Jesus Christ and disciple others. The Great Commission literally changed the first-century world, and it can and will work today!

"Philosophers," wrote Karl Marx, "have only *interpreted* the world differently; the point is, however, to *change* it."

Our concern is that the changed world comes about as the consequence of changed people. Philosophers may produce new philosophies, but only people who have been truly regenerated and are living a Christlike life-style have the keys to a society that can really be changed and become new!

We must widen the circle of faith so that it includes more and more people who have trusted Christ as Lord and Saviour. But how do we go forward with such a plan? How do we become the people who can really change this world? How can we be the people of hope in a hopeless world?

2

The Kingdoms of This World Vs. The Kingdom of God

Handel penned a song that has become immortal because it expresses a Biblical truth:

> *The kingdoms of this world are become,*
> *The kingdoms of our Lord, and of His Christ;*
> *And He shall reign forever and ever,*
> *King of kings! And Lord of lords!*

Are we really living in a new, more powerful age of Satan? Is the kingdom of this world the all-powerful pervading influence on mankind?

Anton LaVey, known as the "High Priest of the First Church of Satan" in San Francisco, stated:

> The Satanic Age started in 1966. That's when God was proclaimed dead, the Sexual Freedom League came into prominence, and the hippies developed as a free sex culture (Arthur Lyons, *The Second Coming: Satanism in America* [New York: Dodd, Mead & Company, 1970]).

This is no time for soft, easy Christianity or uncommitted Christians! Today we are engaged in an all-out battle to the finish. The forces of evil are arrayed against the forces of good and God!

Look at the Big Picture

To understand the big picture in this battle for the souls of men, we must go back into history. The roots of the conflict predate even the creation of man.

15

In the oldest Book of the Bible, Job, we discover some thought-provoking information about the early days of our planet and the surrounding universe:

> Where wast thou when I laid the foundations of the earth? Declare, if thou hast understanding. Who hath laid the measures thereof, if thou knowest? Or who hath stretched the line upon it? Whereupon are the foundations thereof fastened? Or who laid the corner stone thereof; when the morning stars sang together, and all the sons of God shouted for joy? (Job 38:4-7).

What interesting terms: "morning stars" and "sons of God." Careful study reveals that these titles refer to angels—spirit creatures that are stronger than man and have a personal audience with God himself. These spirit beings are depicted as "shouting for joy" at the creation of the universe! What a beautiful picture of harmony and oneness of purpose—no fighting, no disagreements, no rebellion. This passage indicates that all was well in heaven and the universe.

In this realm, the most exalted position next to the Godhead belonged to a perfect creature called Lucifer. The prophet Ezekiel describes him as the "king of Tyre" (Ezekiel 28:11) who is the power behind the "prince of Tyre" that is prophesied against in verses 1 and 2:

> The word of the Lord came again unto me, saying, Son of man, say unto the prince of Tyrus, Thus saith the Lord God; Because thine heart is lifted up, and thou hast said, I am a god, I sit in the seat of God, in the midst of the seas; yet thou art a man, and not God, though thou set thine heart as the heart of God.

As the prophet continues, it becomes clear that he is describing Lucifer:

> Moreover the word of the Lord came unto me, saying, Son of man, take up a lamentation upon the king of Tyrus, and say unto him, Thus saith the Lord God; Thou sealest up the sum, full of wisdom, and perfect in beauty. Thou hast been in Eden the garden of God; every precious stone

was thy covering, the sardius, topaz, and the diamond, the beryl, the onyx, and the jasper, the sapphire, the emerald, and the carbuncle, and gold: the workmanship of thy tabrets and of thy pipes was prepared in thee in the day that thou wast created. Thou art the anointed cherub that covereth; and I have set thee so: thou wast upon the holy mountain of God; thou hast walked up and down in the midst of the stones of fire. Thou wast perfect in thy ways from the day that thou wast created, till iniquity was found in thee (Ezekiel 28:11-15).

Lucifer is shown as the most beautiful, the wisest, and the most exalted of all God's creation. He had God's "seal of perfection" and was the "anointed cherub that covereth." He was the picture of perfection. (Remember, the Godhead was not created, but has always existed.)

Then Ezekiel gives us the pivotal point of all history. Lucifer was perfect in all his ways *until* unrighteousness was found in [him]" (28:15, *NASB*). At this precise point in history, Lucifer fell and became "Satan."

Another Old Testament prophet, Isaiah, tells us exactly what Lucifer's sin was:

How art thou fallen from heaven, O Lucifer, son of the morning! how art thou cut down to the ground, which didst weaken the nations! For thou hast said in thine heart, I will ascend into heaven, I will exalt my throne above the stars of God: I will sit also upon the mount of the congregation, in the sides of the north: I will ascend above the heights of the clouds; I will be like the Most High. Yet thou shalt be brought down to hell, to the sides of the pit. They that see thee shall narrowly look upon thee, and consider thee, saying, Is this the man that made the earth to tremble, that did shake kingdoms. . . . But thou art cast out (Isaiah 14:12-16, 19).

In the original Hebrew, this narrative is like a song of sorrow; God is mourning over this beautiful, perfect being that He had created and loved. Because of Lucifer's pride, sin and suffering were introduced into the universe. Five times in these verses, it is recorded that Lucifer said in his heart, "I will . . . "—the expression of his rebellion against God. Lucifer wanted God to move over and make room for him; he wanted to become God!

Look again at verse 16 in *The Living Bible:* "Everyone there will stare at you and ask, 'Can this be the one who shook the earth and the kingdoms of the world?' " This question carries with it a sense of unbelief. We will ultimately have the opportunity of seeing Lucifer in his defeated final state, and we will look askance, unable to believe that anything so puny and powerless was able to wreak such havoc on this world.

In Revelation 12 we learn more about Lucifer's sin and downfall. Apparently there was a great rebellion throughout the universe, as Lucifer enticed one-third of the angels to follow him in his revolt against God. And the beautiful universe God had created was now contaminated by the worst pollutant—sin. God pronounced judgment on Satan and all the angels who had followed him in his rebellion.

Jesus said the place of eternal banishment has already been prepared for Satan: "Depart from me, ye cursed, into everlasting fire, *prepared for the devil and his angels*" (Matthew 25:41). By implication, hell was not created as a repository for any human being, but for a rebellious devil and his sinful, fallen angels.

We must remember that Satan is only a created being. And, even though one-third of the angels followed him and fell, two-thirds of the heavenly host did not sin. So, God's forces still outnumber Satan's forces by at least two to one! Of course, God is himself infinitely greater than Satan! No wonder John wrote: "Greater is he that is in you, than he that is in the world" (1 John 4:4).

Earth Becomes the Focal Point of the Battle

Attention was then focused on the planet "earth." Some people speculate that the earth became "void" (Genesis 1:2) or that it experienced some catastrophe that destroyed what had been. Then God beautified it and earth was to become the next arena for the greatest contest of all time. The battle between light and darkness, good and evil, righteousness and unrighteousness, God and Satan, would take place here.

"So God created man in his own image. . . . And God saw everything that he had made, and, behold, it was very good"

(Genesis 1:27, 31). Mankind now is the focus of attention in the most fascinating drama ever to unfold.

Even though self-will had been the root cause of sin and disruption in heaven, God still created mankind with a free will. God's will was perfect. Then Lucifer exercised his will against God in rebellion—and there were two wills diametrically opposed to each other. Now, with the creation of Adam and Eve, there were two more wills in existence. At first, they were in harmony with God; creation and Creator were as one. . . .

But it didn't last long. When Lucifer rebelled he was thrown out of heaven, and when Adam and Eve were tempted and fell, they were thrown out of the Garden of Eden, "lest [they] put forth [their] hand, and take also of the tree of life, and eat, and live for ever" (Genesis 3:22).

God Always Has a Plan

But God was not caught without a plan! Isn't that a beautiful, exciting thought? The first prophetic promise in the Bible is recorded in Genesis 3:15: "And I [God] will put enmity between thee and the woman, and between thy seed and her seed; it shall bruise thy head, and thou shalt bruise his heel." This has direct reference to Christ's death at Calvary and His resurrection. The enemy, Satan, would inflict a wound that would not be fatal, but he would himself receive a mortal head wound.

Satan is already a defeated foe! "Ye are of God . . . and have overcome them: because greater is he that is in you, than he that is in the world" (1 John 4:4). But just who or what have we overcome? The preceding verse tells us we have overcome the "spirit of antichrist" or the spirit of this world system. The battle between God and Satan is still raging on our planet, but we know the outcome!

> And the devil that deceived them was cast into the lake of fire and brimstone, where the beast and the false prophet are, and shall be tormented day and night for ever and ever (Revelation 20:10).

There, we've read it from the very last Book of the Bible and we already know the outcome! Utter defeat and eternal banishment are in store for Satan! But, in the meantime, we are in the midst of a battle that is being waged here on earth and in the soul of every person.

Out of Satan's rebellion and Adam and Eve's sin, this world system came into existence. Adam, who had been entrusted with the power to rule over everything on earth, gave his "power of attorney" to Satan. And, by this act, he passed on to all people a spiritual death, for which the only cure is the blood of the Lamb. Jesus called Satan the "ruler of this world" (John 12:31, *RSV*). The moment man disobeyed God, he lost his spiritual life and his communion with God was cut off.

Satan won round one in the Garden. But, thanks be to God, the battle is not over yet! It has just begun for our generation. We are part of this ancient battle between God and Satan. Mankind fell, but God took immediate action with His plan of redemption to buy mankind back from a hopeless situation. God's plan was to come to earth himself, in the form of His Son, live among men, and then die for them. But He would not be kept captive by death! God set aside His divine rights for a time and was subjected to temptation. Then, as the sinless Substitute, He died to pay the price of redemption.

God's plan, as executed by His Son, is described by the apostle Paul:

> For when we were yet without strength, in due time Christ died for the ungodly. For scarcely for a righteous man will one die: yet peradventure for a good man some would even dare to die. But God commendeth his love toward us, in that, while we were yet sinners, Christ died for us. Much more then, being now justified by his blood, we shall be saved from wrath through him. For if, when we were enemies, we were reconciled to God by the death of his Son; much more, being reconciled, we shall be saved by his life (Romans 5:6-10).

The resurrection of Jesus Christ was the one event that sealed Satan's doom! Jesus is alive, and all who believe in Him are declared to be righteous before God. Satan has no legal hold or authority over the true believer!

This is the background for the battle between the kingdom of Satan and the kingdom of God.

Where Do You Fit Into This Battle?

Where do you stand in this battle of the ages? On which side have you decided to live? Who or what has control of your life? Today's battleground is the human soul, mind, and body. Yes, the battle takes place in every human being.

Think back to the moment you accepted Jesus Christ as Lord and Saviour and depended on Him to release you from bondage to sin. As a child of God, your first desire was to live a life pleasing to Him. It probably seemed like a simple thing to do; an easy transition to make. But very quickly you discovered it is a battle on three fronts—the world, the flesh, and the devil. A major part of any battle is planning strategy. Strategists study carefully famous battles of the past to gain guidance in handling current conflicts correctly and to the best advantage.

Paul talks about the "flesh" trap and lists the following carnal activities:

> Now the works of the flesh are manifest, which are these, adultery, fornication, uncleanness, lasciviousness, idolatry, witchcraft, hatred, variance, emulations, wrath, strife, seditions, heresies, envyings, murders, drunkenness, revelings, and such like: of the which I tell you before, as I have also told you in time past, that they which do such things shall not inherit the kingdom of God (Galatians 5:19-21).

This is not a pretty picture, but the power of the flesh in a person's life can be defeated and neutralized because of Jesus Christ. (See Romans 6 and 8.) Christ has already won the victory! The Christian is to acknowledge it and live in this victory!

The word *world* in the Bible is most often used to translate the Greek word *kosmos*. This term is used in three ways. First, it is employed to describe the *physical* earth, the planet earth. Second, *kosmos* can refer to *the inhabitants of the earth* in general, as in: "For God so loved the world [*kosmos*, population] that he gave his only begotten Son" (John 3:16).

And third, this Greek word is used to describe this *world system;* a system that operates without God and is opposed to all that is true and of God.

This world system is "humanistic" and embraces such things as culture, art, philosophy, music, science, religion, and pleasure. These things are not evil in themselves, but Satan has cleverly woven them into a system that takes the heart of man away from God. This world system is under Satan's control, and he uses it to divert God's finest creation from having a true relationship with God; encouraging man to focus on that which is temporal and material.

This World System Comes Into Existence

Genesis 4 records the beginning of this system, which is based on man's pride and rejection of God's truth. Cain developed a civilization and culture without God: "And Cain went out from the presence of the Lord, and dwelt in the land of Nod" (Genesis 4:16). Advancements followed and agriculture flourished: "Jabal . . . was the father of such as dwell in tents, and of such as have cattle" (v. 20). Art, music, and culture were introduced: "Jubal . . . was the father of all such as handle the harp and organ" (v. 21). Industry also became a part of this early system: 'Tubalcain [was] an instructor of every artificer in brass and iron" (v. 22).

Don't get me wrong. These things were not evil in themselves, but man's attitude toward them was wrong. He had determined that he could get along without God, and his achievements left God out of his life. In fact, he made himself and his accomplishments a substitute for the true and living God.

This first world system was shot through and through with materialism, pride, violence, and all kinds of evil.

> And it repented the Lord that he had made man on the earth and it grieved him at his heart. And the Lord said, I will destroy man whom I have created from the face of the earth . . . for it repenteth me that I have made them" (Genesis 6:6,7).

As you have been reading these accounts, have any parallels

come to mind? Would God have to apologize for destroying some ancient civilizations if He were to allow this old world to continue the way it is much longer?

Matthew 24:37 tells us: "As the days of Noah were, so shall also the coming of the Son of man be." Pervading the Christian community today is the conviction that we are living in the last days—the days immediately preceding God's intervention in judgment on this earth and its ungodly inhabitants!

The story that unfolds in Genesis 4 is without any hope until the very last verse: "He called his name Enos: then began men to call upon the name of the Lord" (4:26).

The Battle Lines Are Drawn

This battle is for keeps. We see it reenacted in each generation and in every person. The lines are drawn and the temptations are the same. The apostle John instructs us:

> Love not the world, neither the things that are in the world. If any man love the world, the love of the Father is not in him. For all that is in the world, the lust of the flesh, and the lust of the eyes, and the pride of life, is not of the Father, but is of the world (1 John 2:15, 16).

And behind this world system is the great deceiver, Satan. He is still seeking to shift our focus from God to the material, from eternity to the present. And he is doing a pretty good job of it in the 20th century—both with people who are rejecting God and sometimes even with some so-called Christians! Our society has a lot of fancy explanations for our evil world. We blame the economy, taxes, the Arabs, the politicians, ecology, poverty, etc.

This is where the Church enters the picture. God has chosen to use the Church to reach this lost world! This is God's only plan for His world; He has no more Sons to send to redeem it. Jesus commissioned the Church with these words:

> I will build my church; and the gates of hell shall not prevail against it. And I will give unto thee the keys of the kingdom of heaven: and whatsoever thou shalt bind on earth shall be bound in heaven. . . . Go ye therefore, and teach all nations (Matthew 16:18, 19; 28:19).

This commissioning was followed by a promise: "But ye shall receive power, after that the Holy Ghost is come upon you: and ye shall be witnesses unto me" (Acts 1:8). These words proved to be the last spoken by Christ before He returned to the right hand of the Father: "And when he had spoken these things, while they beheld, he was taken up" (Acts 1:9).

So the Church is faced with the task of taking on this present world system and presenting to people a message that can change lives, that can lift them from the depths of sin and start them in a new direction.

"But," you may be asking, "how can we accomplish this task? How can my church be a factor in this battle?"

I thought you'd never ask! Let's look at one of the greatest battles ever waged by a man—young David's victory over the giant Goliath. Before David even met the giant in the valley, he proclaimed: "The battle is the Lord's" (1 Samuel 17:47)! So we look beyond the battle of the present to the promise of victory, knowing that we are not alone: "If God be for us, who can be against us?" (Romans 8:31).

Since we are in a battle, we need weapons with which to wage war. Paul, under the direction of the Holy Spirit, wrote:

> For though we walk in the flesh, we do not war after the flesh: For the weapons of our warfare are not carnal, but mighty through God to the pulling down of strongholds (2 Corinthians 10:3, 4).

The battle lines have been drawn and it's the kingdom of God versus the kingdom of this world. God and Satan, flesh and blood, the spiritual and the carnal, ignorance and truth, are locked in mortal combat, and the battleground is the hearts and lives of people. As believers, we are in a fight to the finish, a glorious, Blood-bought, final triumph. We are a battleground as well as the offensive weapons God wants to use in His battle! We are the instruments of righteousness!

God Does Battle for His People

If we look at any of the battles in which God fought for His people, we will see He always used some person (or group of people) through whom was released His power by an act of faith. To illustrate this principle, let's consider one of the greatest victories ever won:

> Now the Philistines assembled to fight with Israel, 30,000 chariots and 6,000 horsemen, and people like the sand which is on the seashore in abundance; and they came up and camped in Michmash. . . . When the men of Israel saw that they were in a strait (for the people were hard pressed), then the people hid themselves. . . . Also some of the Hebrews crossed the Jordan into the land of Gad and Gilead. But as for Saul, he was still in Gilgal, and all the people followed him trembling (1 Samuel 13:5-7, NASB).

Jonathan, Saul's son, had triggered this confrontation by his previous invasion of the "garrison of the Philistines that was in Geba, [for] the Philistines heard of it" (1 Samuel 13:3). To compound the problem, Saul's army was shrinking daily, and when he "numbered the people that were present with him, [there were] about six hundred men" (v. 15). That would make the odds at least 100 to 1! Furthermore, they had no weapons with which to fight (v. 22)!

But Jonathan wasn't disheartened, for he was a man of great faith and courage. Jonathan and his armor bearer decided to secretly cross over to the Philistines' garrison: "Come, let's go over to the outpost of those uncircumcised fellows. Perhaps the Lord will act in our behalf. Nothing can hinder the Lord from saving, whether by many or by few (14:6, NIV). And the two of them killed 20 Philistines! Then God caused an earthquake and panic broke out among the entire Philistine army! When Saul and the Israelites realized what was happening, they "rushed out to the battle and found the Philistines killing each other, and there was terrible confusion everywhere. . . . So the Lord saved Israel that day" (14:20, 23, The Living Bible).

God still works through dedicated people who are willing to turn their faith loose. As believers, we must be willing to let God use us to reach a lost and dying world. While it's true that "if God be for us, who can be against us?" (Romans 8:31), this in no way relieves us of our responsibility. We must become the people through whom the Lord can work, to build His church and reach this generation with the gospel, snatching men and women from Satan's stronghold. No matter what part we play or where we fit into the body of Christ, we must always keep uppermost in our thoughts that together we are building the kingdom of God!

The late songwriter, Haldor Lillenas, wrote the following challenge:

Soldiers of Immanuel, go forward in His name,
Holy warfare waging, pow'r of sin engaging;
Lift His royal standard and His truth divine proclaim,
Till the world shall own Him King.

Chorus:

Go forth, go forth, and battle for the right,
Defeat the foe and put his host to flight;
Ye soldiers of Immanuel, press on
Until the victory is won!

3

What Is Our Mission?

Are we faced with a "mission possible" or a "mission impossible"? Was the Lord really serious about reaching the world in a single generation? Is it possible to accomplish this task in our lifetime, or must it be left to another generation?

Before you answer, let's consider that our task is to reach more than 4 *billion* people! Not 4 million, but 4 billion! A billion is not 10 times or 100 times greater than a million, but 1,000 times more!

Let me illustrate the difference between a million and a billion like this: Suppose your wife came to you and asked for $1 million to spend at the rate of $1,000 per day. It would take her about 3 years to spend the $1 million. But suppose she asked for $1 billion to spend at the same rate of $1,000 per day. You wouldn't see her again for about 3,000 years!

About the only things we measure in the billions are the national debt, the gross national product, and the world population.

Jesus said, "I will build my church . . ." (Matthew 16:18). And the Church is still the vehicle God uses to communicate the gospel. Our specific mission is stated in Mark 16:15: "Go ye into all the world, and preach the gospel to every creature." Jesus also gave a promise for our day: "This gospel of the kingdom shall be preached in all the world for a witness unto all nations; and then shall the end come" (Matthew 24:14).

Our Mission

"Our mission" has the sound of a challenge, the excitement of intrigue, the possibility of victory, and is a job that must be done!

"Our mission" is a mandate that cannot be ignored or shrugged off. Every soldier's desire is to hear at the end of the battle, "Well done!" Paul spoke about "fighting the good fight."

"Our mission" emphasizes that you and I together are the basic link in this chain of strategy and mission.

In the past, we may have made an honest consecration to the Lord to be part of this great harvest. We made this commitment in all sincerity, but upon leaving that place of consecration—the emotion of battle enlistment past—we were totally overwhelmed with the task. We were swamped with the problem of where to start, how to start, and with whom to start. About that time the enemy of our soul whispered, "Why don't you just put it off until a better time? After all, it's really too great a task for one person to handle. . . ."

So, once again, we were stirred by the challenge to be a productive Christian, but we didn't follow through with any kind of action. We went down in defeat one more time and became laden with guilt about not witnessing.

The Plan Christ Used

Jesus, our "Commander in chief," has a plan that worked in His day. And His plan enables any generation to reach its world with His message of hope.

Christ selected 12 disciples, associated with them, consecrated them, gave them His example to follow, and delegated responsibility to them. Then He supervised and watched them move into lives of full reproduction. And, with these 12, after they were turned loose in the harvest and endowed with the power of the Holy Spirit, He changed the world! So effective were they that the world complained about the impact they were having: "These men have turned the world upside down" (Acts 17:6, *RSV*).

By this world's standards it wasn't a very grandiose scheme. In fact, these men became objects of scorn. Twelve against the world—yet the world cried "uncle"!

Changed people can change this world! Jesus selected 12 men, gave himself to them as the Example, and taught them. And, after they had spent 3 years with the Master, they were turned loose to carry on His message. It is a simple plan, but one that still works effectively today.

The World Can Be Reached in This Generation

Theoretically, the world can be reached in our generation or any generation that will put into practice the principles of Jesus! What has gone wrong with the harvest? Why are we still faced with this task of world evangelism? Is the problem with the preceding generation? Can we pinpoint the weakness or failure that caused the plan to break down?

There was an urgency about Jesus: "I *must* be about my Father's business" (Luke 2:49). Is it possible that we have been sidetracked from our number one priority? We could spend all our time asking questions, but the important thing is not to question, but to get on with the task; not to fix blame, but to begin moving for God. We have not been saved to have a free ride to glory on flowery beds of ease. We are in a battle! We have a mission! We are under a directive!

The reality that we face is no match for the neatness of theory. And we have no excuses that will stand the test of the "Judgment Seat" scrutiny of Christ. God has given us ample instruction in the Word about the responsibility of a steward. (Note: the Parable of the Dishonest Steward in Luke 16; the Parable of the Pounds in Luke 19; the Parable of the Talents in Matthew 25; and Jesus' warning about the unfaithful servant in Luke 12.)

Let us put aside all the excuses that have been used in the past. There are *no* impossible situations! There is *no* situation that is insurmountable to the Church marching under orders from the King of kings. The world can be reached in our generation with the plan given to us by Jesus Christ.

The Crisis Facing Christianity

Let's look at the harvest in more detail and outline the task confronting us. It has been described as "*the* crisis facing Christianity." Every day about 345,000 people are born and 146,000 people die. This translates into a net gain of 138 people per minute, 199,000 per day, 6 million per month, and 72 million each year!

Demographers, the people who plot and project growth and population patterns, estimate that 250 million people were alive in Jesus' day. This number doubled by the year 1650, and then doubled again to 1 billion people by 1850. Eighty years later, in 1930, the earth had 2 billion inhabitants. Notice how the time it takes for the population to double shortens with each increase. In 1975, the population exploded to 4 billion and, in less than 35 years, it is projected there will be 8 billion people on our planet!

This population explosion is happening worldwide, but it is concentrated in urban areas. It took from Adam until today to accumulate the first 4 billion, but it will take only 35 years for the next 4 billion to be added to that total. It will happen in less than a single generation—our generation!

Just to keep up with this increase, everything will have to double—hospitals, food, housing, doctors, missionaries, churches, and preachers!

So the world population will have doubled by the year 2010—what else is new? We are not shocked by such news. But think of it like this: If there had been only 12 people on earth when Christ was born, and they had multiplied at *our* rate of increase, there would now be over 1 *trillion*—seven persons for every square foot of land!

It is estimated that 2,000 people in our world starve to death every hour of every day. That adds up to 50,000 per day and 18 million per year! Robert S. McNamara, president of the World Bank, warns that the population explosion is as great a threat to the survival of civilization as the nuclear bomb.

Suppose we could choose mass migration as the solution to this explosion of people. If we built spaceports in Moscow, Calcutta, Peking, and New York, and put 100 people on each spaceship leaving each spaceport every 3 minutes around the clock, this would get rid of the daily gain in population. But, at this rate, in less than 50 years we would have populated the moon, Venus, Mercury, Mars, the moons of Jupiter, and Saturn to the same density as on earth!

The challenge facing the Church is to reach these lost people with the gospel. And the Church is composed of *you* and *me!* Yes, you already know that, but this is a reminder that the responsibility translates right down to you and me. We are faced with two choices: We can either get on with this task of reaching the lost, or we can begin thinking up reasons to give the Master on Judgment Day when He asks why we didn't obey His command.

The Mandate Is to Reach Every Person

In Mark's version of the Great Commission there is one significant detail that is not as evident in the other Gospels. Mark 16:15 says: "Go ye into all the world, and preach the gospel to *every creature.*" Keep in mind that there are about 138,000 more lost people in the world this morning than there were yesterday, and when you go to church this coming Sunday there will be about 1 million more people without Christ than there were last Sunday.

To reach "every creature" will require some drastic changes in our personal life-styles. The priorities of our churches must change! As members of a local church, *we* must change our thinking, too. We can no longer conduct church "as usual." When this year ends, there will be about 50 million more people that need to be reached with the gospel. And, at our present rate, Christianity is not even keeping pace with the population growth.

How many of the 146,000 people who will die today will go to hell without having heard about Jesus Christ? This flow of immortal souls into an eternal hell should cause us intense concern! But what about the 345,000 babies born in that same 24 hours—will they live and die and also go to eternal damnation without hearing the gospel of good news? Today, there are approximately nine times as many people who have not heard about Jesus Christ as the total population of the world when Christ stated His Great Commission.

Picture it this way: If we lined up all the people in this world who are without Christ, they would make a line that would circle the globe 30 times! And the line grows 20 miles longer each day! If we were to drive down that line and give each person a gospel tract or Bible, at the rate of 50 miles per hour, 10 hours a day, 7 days a week, it would take 4 years and 40 days to reach the end of the original line. But by then the line would have grown another 30,000 miles!

It seems as though we have been sidetracked from our primary task. Mark reminds us that "every creature" should have at least one opportunity in his lifetime to hear the gospel presented and then make a decision—either yes or no.

Jesus said some things that I do not understand, but the Great Commission is not one of them. How can you or I explain it away? This was His last commandment! Jesus stated: "If ye love me, keep my commandments" (John 14:15). And John wrote: "Hereby we do know that we know him, if we keep his commandments" (1 John 2:3). Wouldn't you agree that this is one commandment we haven't yet fulfilled? It is time that we be about this divine imperative!

Let's Look at Our Own Numbers

According to a *Christianity Today* Gallup poll (December 21, 1979, pp. 12-14), 53 percent of the people who live in America claim a born-again experience, and 19 percent of the population claim to be Pentecostal or charismatic. That's exciting, but it means about half our population, 110 million people, are still without Christ!

Now let's look at how well the Assemblies of God has done. According to the "annual church ministries report" for 1979 (the last year available), we won 163,780 people to Christ in our churches. That's exciting! We also had a growth rate over the past decade of about 63 percent, which is phenomenal among church groups in our day. Most churches are standing still or losing membership.

Let's pretend we could stop the clock at high noon and make everything come to a standstill. The cemeteries would be locked and all the obstetrical wards of our hospitals would close down. No one else would be born or die until we (the Assemblies of God) have won to Christ all those people in America who aren't born again. At our present rate (1979 figures), it would take about 671 years to get the job done! But this doesn't take into account the growth in population that's occurring!

In 1979, our overseas churches won 363,810 to the Lord. So, together we reached 527,590 people with the gospel and they accepted Christ as Lord and Saviour. But just compare those figures with the world population and calculate how long it would take us at our present rate to reach "planet earth's" inhabitants for Christ. We have our backs against the wall! It's not a rosy picture. In fact, it may be downright tragic, for we have had the scope of our mission so graphically portrayed to us.

It Is a Job That Can Be Done

Is it a hopeless job? We have one criterion by which we can measure our task—the New Testament Church. We discover that the Early Church came the closest to reaching their world in their own generation. The geographical borders of that church were phenomenal. After a few short years, there were Christians in Rome, Galatia, Philippi, and other places. Just take your Bible atlas and mark off the churches of that era. You will see that by the end of the first century, the Mediterranean Sea had become a "Christian" lake! All this happened in spite of the barriers of time and distance. Remember, it took about 5 days to walk the 75 miles from Jerusalem to Nazareth.

The growth pattern was exciting and explosive. First there was Jesus himself, then there were 12, then 70, then 120 in the Upper Room, then 3,000 on the Day of Pentecost, and 5,000 more in Jerusalem (and that number didn't include women and children)! At that point the Bible speaks of *multiplication*, not just addition!

This growth of believers spread throughout the Roman Empire and to the ends of the civilized world—within about two generations! This is an example to us that it can be done again in our sophisticated world. The growth of the Early Church occurred during periods of intense persecution and extreme hardships. But the believers persevered in spite of a society that was downright hostile to the message and the messengers. Without a doubt, the New Testament Church experienced the greatest expansion any church has ever seen. Let's make it happen again!

Jesus Christ is still the same. The gospel has not lost its power to change people, and multitudes are hungry and longing for the Bread of Life. We have methods available to us that the first church couldn't have even imagined. And there are more of us than the 3,000 or 5,000 who were saved in the earliest days of the Church. We are an army ready to be totally mobilized.

Examine Your Concepts

We must turn from our concept of *addition* of souls to New Testament *multiplication.* If we in the Assemblies of God, with our 1½ million people, were to multiply ourselves and double our size every year, in 10 years we would number 768 million! It can be done! Could you, if you really made an all-out effort, win at least one person to Christ each year for the next 10 years? Sure you could! And if each person who is presently a part of the Assemblies of God did the same, we could totally change this nation!

Now that is just here in America. If the Assemblies of God churches overseas (which number about 7 million strong) were to double themselves every year, in 10 years that number would explode to over 3.5 billion! The world population today is about 4.5 billion.

Multiplication is a New Testament concept: "And in those days, when the number of the disciples was *multiplied . . .*" (Acts 6:1). The 3,000 and the 5,000 had been *added* to the original 120 in the Upper Room (Acts 2:41; 4:4), but things were happening so rapidly that the Holy Spirit no longer added, but multiplied the number of believers. And multiplication is a much faster process of increasing the numbers in any mathematical equation.

We glibly give vocal assent that our God can do anything, then settle back into our comfortable rut of doing things like we've always done them. There are, however, indications that many of our churches are experiencing explosive growth. They have discovered the secret of New Testament multiplication and outreach and are believing God for the harvest.

This is too critical a day and too many souls hang in the balance between everlasting life and death for us to go on having "regular services." I'm not knocking orderly services, but the Great Commission was Christ's final command and we need to realize the importance of obeying it. In the past, this has been the number one failure of our church, but that need no longer be the case. The time has come for us to lay aside all the innovations, trimmings, frills, and anything else that might distract us from our main task of taking the gospel to "every creature." We must address ourselves to this divine imperative!

The chorus of the song "Our Mission," written by Margot Zilch, was dedicated to the 1968 "Council on Evangelism," but it still has a message for us today:

> *'Til the world shall hear.*
> *Bound in sin and fear.*
> *Our mission never ending,*
> *'Til the world shall hear.*

4

Every Believer Must Be Part of the Harvest

During World War II a guest was to tour a munitions and weapons factory. As he walked through the main gate with his guide, he noticed a large sign above the gate with "IADOM" written in large letters. It didn't seem to make any sense to the guest, but he went on. Inside he saw the same sign in miniature over each doorway through which they walked and over each work location—nothing more, only "IADOM." Curiosity finally overcame him and he asked his guide, "What does the sign mean? I've seen them everywhere in your factory."

The guide replied: "We had to do something to impress on our employees the importance of their job whether it is large or small, important or insignificant. You see, a simple error or slip in assembly could place a soldier's life in jeopardy and weaken our cause. The letters stand for the slogan, 'It All Depends on Me'!"

Every Believer Is Needed

For any harvesting to take place, every believer must be battle-ready, motivated, and equipped for the task. Furthermore, each believer must realize he is important to the mission. It has been too easy for the church to relegate the task of reaching the lost to the professional clergy and missionaries. "After all, we are paying them to reach the lost and to do the ministry!" is a sentiment that is often thought and sometimes expressed.

Every believer is to be a participant in the harvest. If God didn't have a divine purpose for us on this earth, He would have called us home to heaven after we accepted His Son as our Saviour. We have been saved to serve and to be workers in the harvest. And no one has an "excuse slip" that will exempt him/her from the harvest field. Every believer has been commissioned, and every believer has been given one or more gifts to be used in the body of Christ for the harvest.

There was no doubt in Jesus' mind about the need of the harvest: "The harvest is so plentiful and the workers so few" (Luke 10:21, *The Living Bible*). The question that was not spelled out, but implied is: "Where are the harvesters?"

Is the harvest really taking place in your church? through your church? Where there is life there will be growth. When the church is alive it will reach beyond itself. Growth and evangelism are the natural fruit of a normal, healthy Christian church. And an active harvest will result in an ever-expanding church.

Develop a Plan That Will Work

We must develop a well thought-out strategy that will, on a day-to-day basis, accomplish the long-range goal of reaching this world. Jesus had a strategy that worked in His day and it will work today.

Let's focus on the principles that determined Christ's methods. The Gospels are the only eyewitness accounts we have of Christ at work and they were written by people who saw the truth and were changed by that truth. As we read the Gospels, Jesus' objective becomes clear: He intended to save out of this world a people for himself. Then He would use these same people to build a Church that would never perish and would be the vehicle for reaching those who were still lost. Never forget this one great fact: Jesus is "the Saviour of the world" (John 4:42). God wants *all* mankind to be saved and to come to a knowledge of the truth.

Jesus' life-style was ordered by His objective. There was nothing frivolous about His life. He always kept His goal in sight: "I must be about my Father's business" (Luke 2:49). He was born, He lived among men, and He died and rose again according to His Father's plan.

The Plan Christ Used

Jesus conceived a plan, not a program, that would not fail. In fact, at a casual reading it may not appear to be a plan because it was so unassuming. It's gone largely unnoticed by many of us who are so busy, and it is different from the long-range or short-range plans of most church organizations. It is so far removed from our context that it could be called revolutionary.

Christ's concern was not with programs that would reach the lost multitudes, but with men and women whom the multitudes would follow. People were His method of winning the world. People who were changed, who had come alive, who had had a life-changing experience; they were the vehicle through which the message would flow. The fruit of evangelism and church growth would be naturally produced by these people. It was to be a natural process. Just as a seed is planted and grows to maturity and bears fruit, so people would be changed into fruit-bearing reproducers of the Kingdom and Kingdom principles.

Jesus started the process by calling a few men to follow Him. Notice this selection was made before He organized an evangelistic campaign. This is the first clue. The men He chose wouldn't really impress us at a first reading. None were prominent leaders or members of the priesthood and none were important personalities. For the most part, they were common ordinary men. They represented a cross section of very average people in any society. By our standards they would be considered a rather motley crew. Were they the people you would have chosen to change the world?

He gave himself to these 12 men, with the intent that these transformed men, molded into the image of the Master, would be the catalyst to change the world. That didn't mean that all others were excluded from following Him. Many followed Him, and this is evident from reading the Gospels. There were the Seventy and the multitudes, but we can sense a lesser priority given to those outside of the chosen 12. Jesus devoted most of His life on earth to these 12 and literally staked His whole future mission on them—it was 3 years of highly intensified training. Jesus was not trying to impress the multitudes, but was getting ready to build a Kingdom and a Church!

An Overlooked Principle

Today, most of our evangelistic efforts begin with the masses with the hope that all who are reached will naturally stay in the church or be conserved in the Kingdom. If this pattern of Jesus' means anything to us, it should emphasize the fact that a foundation must be laid in the beginning upon which an effective outreach can be built. This means training people "for the work of the ministry" (Ephesians 4:12). Jesus concentrated His life and efforts, while at the same time not neglecting the multitudes. Everything that was done with the Twelve was done in love and for the people who would be reached in the future.

This principle of concentration has been demonstrated to be effective in our modern-day world by the Communists who have, in large measure, adopted it. They have multiplied from a handful of zealots under Lenin about a hundred years ago into a vast company of followers who today enslave more than half the people of this world! They have demonstrated that the multitudes can easily be won through people who are sold-out zealots to a cause. The spread of the vicious doctrine of Communistic thought is an indictment upon our church and lifestyles. If they can do it, we can do it! We have such a flabby commitment to world evangelism and treat it as though it were something we could choose to do or forget.

Let's lift some principles from the life and training process that Jesus used to prepare the Twelve:

The First Step: Availability

In our concern to reach the lost we have launched one crash program after another without realizing that we must begin with a priority on training the present church we have. Then we must use these who have been mobilized to reach out. We must again realize that anyone who is willing to follow Christ can become a powerful influence in this world.

So we must start with the first question: "Are you available to Jesus Christ?" And in the kingdom of heaven availability always counts for more than ability. The first step, then, is recruiting for training the people we already have.

The Second Step: Association

Jesus followed His selection by spending quality time with His followers in "presence" or association. It was a process of letting them gain knowledge by observation before it was understood by explanation. The wisdom of this strategy is noted in the fact that a single living message is worth at least a hundred explanations. Jesus made it clear that before these were to "cast out devils" or "to preach deliverance to the captives" they were to be with Him.

There is no substitute for being with Jesus! In today's busy world it's easy to let our own personal devotional time with the Master become secondary. For ministry to develop out of character there is nothing that can take the place of our daily Bible reading, meditation, and personal prayer life. When will we really learn this lesson? Preaching to the masses, which is a necessity, is in itself never enough by way of preparation to work in the harvesting of souls. Here is where each member of the body of Christ can make preparation.

This principle, sharing quality time with Jesus, is such a simple process that we tend to overlook it. But effective ministry can only grow out of that personal relationship spent in His presence. The question to ask yourself is: "Have you been spending time with Him in private devotions?" This has been a look at the second principle.

The Third Step: Consecration

The people who responded to the call to follow Jesus were not expected to be smart, but He did require them to be obedient and loyal. They were first called "disciples," from which we get our word *discipline,* which really meant that they were "pupils" of the Man. It was much later that they became known as "Christians" (Acts 11:26). Jesus had asked them to follow Him—not to make bold declarations. To follow Him seemed an easy thing to do, but that was because they hadn't followed Him very far. It soon became evident that being a disciple would involve more than a good time; it would mean a complete, total surrender and submission to Him. Many of the past habits and thinking patterns would have to be changed to conform to the new (Matthew 5:1-12; Luke 16:13).

There was a cross to be faced! Many followed Him until they were overshadowed by the fact of the cross. Many were numbered with Him as long as He passed out the bread to fill their stomachs, but when Jesus talked of the sacrifice necessary, "many of his disciples went back, and walked no more with him" (John 6:66). Note that Jesus did not go running after them to persuade them to stay a little longer with Him. He was preparing leaders for the Kingdom and each must willingly pay the price of consecration.

Jesus didn't persuade them to make their commitments to His teachings or His plans but to himself, to a person. Out of this we discover that obedience can be seen by the expression of love, "If ye love me . . ." (John 14:15, 21, 23, 24; 15:10, 12). Love was to be expressed in life-action. The cross in the life of Christ was the climax of Jesus' consecration to do the will of His Father. It showed that obedience cannot be compromised . . . there must be a commitment unto death. You'll note, too, that the disciples were not moved to this place of commitment until they had the privilege of following Him for a period of time.

We are engaged in a war! The issues are life and death, heaven or hell, salvation or damnation! This is a lesson that must be learned again and again in our wishy-washy, easy-living kind of world. We can no longer be indifferent to this aspect of Christian living. It demands a giving without reservation. The question to ask yourself is: "Are you willing, today, to make a complete total consecration of your will and life to obey His will?" So we have looked at principle number three.

The Fourth Step: Being Spirit-Filled

Look at Christ's earthly life and you will discover it was a life of giving. He gave what the Father had given Him. He gave peace (John 14:27); He gave joy in the midst of trouble (John 15:11); He gave keys to the Kingdom (John 16:19); He gave His own glory (John 17:22, 24); and He gave the Holy Spirit (John 20:22). And He's given all of these to us, also! But the most beautiful expression of the love that gives is: "God so loved the world, that he gave his only begotten Son" (John 3:16).

In turn, the followers of Jesus, who had received so freely, were to give as freely as they had received (Matthew 10:8); they were to love as He had loved them (John 13:34, 35). Love became the standard and they saw this demonstrated in Jesus with the culmination at Calvary. Such a demonstration through the followers of Christ would shout at the world the fact that the gospel is for real and is the truth.

Those disciples, like us, needed an experience with Christ that was so real that their lives would be filled with His presence in such a way that they would not question this reality. Evangelism had to become a burning, flaming, compulsion— and nothing less than a personal baptism in the Holy Spirit would be sufficient (Luke 24:49; Acts 1:4, 5, 8; 2:1-4)!

We are faced with a superhuman task, world evangelism, and it can be accomplished only by a supernatural indwelling of the Holy Spirit. So the next question to ask yourself is: "Have you received your personal infilling of the Holy Spirit since you believed?" This has been the fourth principle of preparation for evangelism.

The Fifth Step: Living It Out

People today are looking for demonstrations of the real thing. Jesus showed His disciples exactly what their life-style should be as He lived His life as their example. It's been said, "Your life speaks so loud that I can't hear a word you are saying!" Jesus let His disciples see Him in His prayer life. More than 20 times in the Gospels you can find the practice of Jesus in prayer, and most of those occasions involved major decisions that had to be faced in His life (Luke 3:21; 6:12; 9:29; etc.). Everything that Jesus did and said had a relevance to the task of evangelism.

The very life-style of Jesus was a continuous sermon. He did not ask anything of His followers that He had not already shown them by His life. People today need living demonstrations of the reality of the gospel. They are not looking for another explanation or more doctrine; they want to see reality in shoe leather. This truth must become a natural part of our life. So the question is: "Is your life a living demonstration of the truth of the gospel?" This has been a look at a principle you already know all about, but are you doing it?

The Sixth Step: Using Your Ability

Every child of God has at least one talent that must be exercised in the body of Christ for the health and outreach of the Body. Paul spoke of this universality of ministries: "Unto *every one of us* is given grace [*charis*] according to the measure of the gift of Christ" (Ephesians 4:7). "The manifestation of the Spirit is *given to every man* to profit withal" (1 Corinthians 12:7).

If you are a believer, you have abilities that have been given to you which are your responsibility to exercise and use for the wholeness of the Body for evangelism. No child of God should have an inferiority complex. You are a gifted child! And for every gift that has been given, the Holy Spirit has also planned how it can best be used for the upbuilding of the Church.

How many talents are assigned to each believer? At least one and perhaps more. You can make the application here from Christ's Parable of the Talents in which one was given five, another two, and another one. (See Matthew 25:14-30.)

"Ye are the body of Christ, and members in particular" (1 Corinthians 12:27). Paul used the picture of the human body—hands, feet, inner parts, eyes, ears— to illustrate the various ministries that are to be used in the Church. These are for service and ministry so that the Body can be healthy. (Too many of us seem to be concerned about being the "mouth.") Spiritual ministries or abilities are for the benefit of others and for the upbuilding (edifying) of the Body.

I believe that we could unlock a tremendous potential for church growth that is now buried, if each believer would begin using his/her gift or talents. No one is excused from the ministry of soul winning, even if he doesn't have a talent for evangelism, because that is an overriding, all-encompassing directive given by Christ.

But in the discovery and use of talents by each believer, the Church becomes a functioning, living organism that is the vehicle of world evangelism. There are two things that the Bible is clear about: (1) God wants each Christian to have and use his God-given gifts and abilities, and (2) He wants every lost sheep to be found and His church to grow! When each believer exercises his ministry and the Church is a totally integrated functioning body, that is the kind of Church that will experience God's blessings!

God distributes talents to churches and individuals. If that be the case, we should gladly accept what God has given us without any pride or envy, and seek to be available for an exercise in these areas. Whatever God has chosen for you or your church, it is a "gift-mix" that will speed the process of growth and outreach when you allow the dynamic of the Holy Spirit to be released in obedience to Jesus Christ, the Lord of the harvest. Your next question to answer is: "Have you discovered and used your talent in the harvest?" We have looked at the sixth principle of utilizing each believer in the harvest.

The Seventh Step: Reproduction

Jesus intended for the disciples and all His followers to reproduce His likeness in and through the Church that was and is being gathered out of this world. Jesus built into His followers the foundation of a Church that would triumph over all the challenges of evil. It started small, but it would grow in size and strength until it would become a tree greater than all the herbs (Matthew 13:32).

It would not be an easy conquest. Some would die in the battle through martyrdom and others would suffer persecution, but His church would be triumphant in the end, for nothing can prevail against it (Matthew 16:18). Jesus' whole evangelistic strategy depended on the obedience and faithfulness of His followers to the task given them.

The biggest test was whether or not His disciples would carry on His work after He had been taken from them. Could they or would they be able to do the job without His bodily presence with them? They had been told that "without me ye can do nothing" (John 15:1-17). Were they successful? Did they carry out His Great Commission?

Secular history tells us that before the end of the first century the then known world had been largely evangelized! The Word indicates that the disciples were to go into the world and win others. Now, as we look back from our perspective, we can conclude that they did their job more effectively than any succeeding generation of Christians!

Our effectiveness can be checked by asking: "Are those who are following us to Christ now leading others to Him and making disciples of them? Is reproduction taking place? Will our work and ministry be self-perpetuating or will it end when we die?"

Early Church history proved that the plan Jesus had implemented really worked. But our times have changed and have become more sophisticated (we think), and we have adopted much more complicated plans and programs to do the job. Christ's methods were not based on organizations, crusades, or programs, but on better people. Until we have people who are committed, filled with the Holy Spirit, trained, and reproducing, none of our methods will work. I guess you could call this chapter a plea to get back to the simple basics that have always worked.

We do not need better methods; we need better people! Jesus is looking for people who really know Him, Christians who feel His passion for this world and are willing to be nothing so that He might be everything. The next question is: "Are you really bearing the fruit of reproduction?" Jesus said: "I have chosen you, and ordained you, that ye should go and bring forth fruit, and that your fruit should remain" (John 15:16). The greatest mark of Christian maturity rests on this question.

It was just about harvesttime in Montana when we dropped in on a ranch house. The mother was baking bread for the harvesters who would be there in a day or two to bring in the wheat. Little Susan, age 3, was playing about her mother's feet. When she got up and walked out the back door, her mother didn't think too much about her leaving. But later, her mother realized with a start that Susan had been gone for about half an hour.

The mother went out the back door and called, "Susan . . . Susaan . . . Suuusaaan!" No answer. She went down to the barn, but no Susan. She looked into the corral, then in the machine shed, but still no little girl.

Panic hit. Adjoining the house was a wheat field. As the mother looked in that direction, she instinctively knew that was where Susan had wandered. It was late afternoon. The mother ran back to the house and beat on the dinner triangle, summoning her husband and the hired help from the field. When they arrived, the dilemma was quickly explained and the men joined the search. It was tough. The wheat was about the same height as little Susan, and her blond hair would blend in with the color of the ripe wheat.

Fear now seized this little search party. Night was falling and still no Susan. Word spread up and down the valley and neighbors began to arrive and join the search. But, eventually, darkness forced them to abandon their search until light. There was no sleep as the search party gathered in the ranch house to comfort that mom and dad. The nights were cool, with the temperature dropping to the 30°s. It was just about dawn and the sky was turning gray as the party set out to search again.

Before they started into that huge field of wheat, one of the neighbors said, "Hold it, let's organize this and do it right. Hold hands and we'll form a line. We will make a sweep all across the field, then turn around and come back in another sweep until we've covered every inch in a systematic way."

This seemed like an excellent plan, for on the previous day it had been a random effort. They hadn't gone very far, perhaps a couple of hundred yards, when a neighbor called out, "I've found her!" The mother and dad ran to that location. The mother got there first and stooped to pick up the cold lifeless body of their precious little girl. But it was too late! The night had been too much for the child; exposure had taken her life.

As the father arrived and the neighbors gathered around, the silence was broken by sobs of sorrow. Finally that sad group began edging toward the house. Then the husband spoke up and said, "I just want to thank you for your help. . . . But I have only one regret, why didn't we organize ourselves and do this last night?"

Today is no time to dillydally with the harvest! Every believer must be mobilized, trained, and reproducing! We can no longer do our thing; we must do *His* thing! "Look on the fields; for they are white already to harvest" (John 4:35)!

5

Evaluating the Harvest

Which of us hasn't been thrilled to see people streaming forward to make a decision in a church service or at a crusade? It's an exciting moment—the invitation, the altar call, thinking of the joy to be experienced by the new converts, singing "Just as I Am." But, have you also wondered how effective that decision really is? Will it last? Will these people become part of the local church? We're down at the bottom line: how effective is our evangelistic effort?

Before we take a longer look at evaluation, let's examine the "decision" as a concept. "Results must be measurable" is a concept to keep in mind. A "decision" in itself is a weak premise; it must be more than only a decision to be lasting. The "decision" must be followed by discipling as well as integrating this person into a local fellowship of believers. There is no other plan with which to reach this world other than a strong local church. "Parachurch" organizations can be of help to strengthen the church, but a strong, vital, caring, loving local church is God's best plan. The church is the arm of evangelism as well as the nursery to help that new Christian achieve maturity.

Effective evangelism has taken place when that person has become a growing, maturing disciple who is able to share Christ with others. The end product of evangelism is not only a decision, but also a process by which each new convert is incorporated into the local church where he will function as a responsible member.

New Believers Should Be Added to the Local Church

So then, if making disciples and fitting them into the Body is

49

the bottom line for evangelism, what results are being produced in our own personal lives and by the efforts of our church? The Book of Acts points out to us again and again that those who believed were added to the Church (Acts 2:41, 42; 6:1, 7). Are new believers being added to our existing fellowships?

Maybe it's no surprise to you, but it was to me that I could not find any data or research on this subject. We generally point to our numbers in Sunday school and note the increases or decreases as a kind of barometer of the job we are doing. The only papers I could find evaluating the results of evangelism were one prepared by Dr. Win Arn on the results of a mass crusade by Billy Graham, and one about the *Here's Life America* program. These were published in the magazine *Church Growth America* (March-April 1980).

It follows that we may have to plow out some new ground in order to really evaluate evangelism in our own churches. If you are doing an adequate job, you need to have some kind of records from which you can make your judgments. Perhaps, after we evaluate our evangelism, we may be forced to start all over again. Remember one thing: methods are not sacred but the message is divine.

Check Your Own Sunday School Records

Take a long look, starting with your own enrollment figures. Andy Anderson has written a book *Where Action Is* (Nashville, TN: Broadman Press, 1976) and based it on the principle that a church will grow as the enrollment of the Sunday school increases. Look at your enrollment figures and compare the names found there to the names on your church membership roll. Do you note any correlation? How many of your Sunday school pupils have matured enough to become bona fide members of your church? Is there a clue here as to our effectiveness? You will also uncover a fallacy here. How many of your church members have matured to the place where they can and are reproducing themselves?

You may discover another situation that calls for your consideration. How many of your new Sunday school enrollees or new church members have come from another congregation?

When we see growth in a numerical sense, are we seeing a reaching of the lost or are we seeing people coming into our fellowships who have been dissatisfied with their former churches? We have raised a whole lot of questions to be considered and we haven't offered you any great solutions. Perhaps this is an area where we need to commission someone to do an in-depth analysis of our local church and come up with some tools with which we can make an evaluation.

The question, "Are we reaching them?" can be answered by looking at our communities. The recent *Christianity Today* Gallup Poll, mentioned in chapter 3, indicates that approximately 53 percent of Americans claim a born-again experience. Impose those figures on your area, let alone the unreached world, and you have some idea of the task still confronting us.

Start With a Personal Evaluation

Maybe our best approach is to begin by taking a personal inventory. Start with the question: "When did I accept Christ?" That shouldn't be too hard, but it's a starting point. Then ask: "How did I become a Christian?" There's another positive clue as to reaching others.

Follow this with another question: "Have I really been or become a true disciple?" In other words, can you chart some progress in your own spiritual journey? Have you moved from the infant "milk" stage to that of greater maturity? Have you become more knowledgeable in the Word? Have you spent quality time with Jesus? Can you lead another person to Christ?

The tragedy that we may discover will, hopefully, shock us! We may find ourselves taking the same first steps over and over again. We are Christian in name but it must be translated into real living. One of the major concerns the apostle Paul had was that Christians exhibit growth and that each person move from being a "babe" to being "spiritual" (1 Corinthians 2:14 to 3:7). The writer of Hebrews says that we should become "teachers" instead of "[needing] that one teach [us] again . . . the first principles" (5:12-14).

Some sort of ultimate question about your Christian maturity could go like this: "Have you reproduced your Christian experience in some other person's life?" It's not enough to know;

are you *doing* what you know should be done? Are you at the
point in your Christian experience where you can "disciple"
another person? You know you have been successful when the
person you have discipled can in turn disciple someone else.

Evaluate Your Sunday School Class

Let's move from the individual personal evaluation of the
harvest to a larger unit of your church—the Sunday school class.

The Sunday school class has been a very effective "small-
group" function of our church as well as a nonthreatening
group dynamic that can help people to mature in their experience with Christ. What happens in this smaller unit of your
church will very much affect the overall growth of your church.
The class that meets on a regular basis is an effective tool to
allow the maturation process to take place. It is in the class
setting of mutual caring for one another that people of the
harvest can be preserved and cared for. It can function much
like a nursery for newborn babes in Christ.

Now to an evaluation of your own class. An honest look must
begin with an adequate recordkeeping system. If you have no
record system, you have no starting point. If you don't have a
record system, rush, don't walk, to get it instituted. Start with
your enrollment records. Are you still going through the
"three-Sundays-in-a-row" thing or do you enroll every interested person the first time he attends? When people belong
they want to attend. A careful reading of this record should
indicate to you the number of people who have been enrolled
and possibly those who are not yet born-again Christians.

Evaluating Christian maturity is not an easy or simple process. We have been taught that we are not to judge one another
(a whole lot of us do it anyway). However, there are some points
of evaluation that can be made. Go over that enrollment record
with the following in mind: Are the people who visit your class
coming back? Do they stay after they have attended? Are they
consistent? Have they made an effort to become a member of
your church? These questions will give you some basic information.

An elderly preacher took me aside while I was in my early
ministry (in fact, I was pastoring my first church) and said, "If

you can get your people to do three things on a daily basis, they'll all make it to heaven!"

My curiosity aroused, I asked, "Please share them with me."

He paused for effect, raised one of his bushy eyebrows, and pointedly said: "Get them to talk to God for 15 minutes each day—that's praying. Let them have God talk to them for 15 minutes daily—that's reading the Word. And have them talk to someone else about God for 15 minutes each day—that's witnessing!" Then he went on, "In all my years of ministry, and that's been a few, I have never seen a single person who has done this on a consistent basis ever leave the faith."

Perhaps we should ask some of these basic questions: Do the people in your class consistently pray? Are they in the Word on a daily basis? Do they witness with conviction and have results?

Do You Have Any Goals in Your Class/Church?

Are you seeing consistent growth? Do you have a goal for growth? May I suggest a simple, easily attainable goal for your class and school? Each class should show a growth rate of at least one per month in average attendance. That's very minimal, but if your class started out with an average attendance of 12, and you used that simple goal, in 1 year your class would have doubled in size! Suppose your school is near the size of the average Assemblies of God church, and you begin with an attendance of 120 and 10 classes. If each class increased an average of only one person per month, in the next year your church would have doubled in size!

Perhaps a survey among the members of your present class would be in order. Ask such questions as: When did you become a Christian? Why are you attending this class? Are you satisfied with the spiritual growth in your own life? What caused you to come to our church in the first place?

As you take a look at the Sunday school class as a unit of evangelism and the catalyst for growth, it will soon become evident that here is an ideal plan for growth. It will become a tool to integrate new people into the fellowship as well as the outreach unit. Right here is an unlimited and untapped potential for growth.

Look at Your Church

Let's look on the church as a whole. God has no other or better plan to reach this world than through the local church. I have a feeling that the decade that lies ahead of us will, in reality, be the "decade of the local church," and we will see unprecedented growth and harvest in and through our local churches!

How do you evaluate the harvest of your church? We can start by taking a look at the harvest field. According to the *Christianity Today* Gallup Poll, better than one-third of the adult population in America, has had a life-changing religious experience. That translates into better than two-thirds who have *not* had such an experience. So, imposing those figures on your community, there are still about two-thirds of the people who are in need of Jesus Christ as their personal Saviour!

Take that a step further by looking at your present attendance figures or your enrollment and calculating the percentage of the harvest yet to be reached. You could probably reduce those figures by being aware that about 40 million go to church weekly and 17 million go more than once per week. Also keep in mind that only 11 percent read the Bible on a daily basis compared to 10 percent who read it on a weekly basis and 7 percent who read it monthly. It's obvious that we have our challenge before us!

Are You Showing Growth?

The first and most important question in checking on the effectiveness of your church's ministry is: *Are you showing measurable growth?* There is nothing bad about being a "small church" as long as you are growing. Every church has had a beginning and the majority were insignificant. If your church is not growing, there is a problem that is stopping growth. Growth should be the most natural thing to happen in your church. Everything that God brought into existence and that is alive grows! If you are not growing, please take a long hard look at some of the things that may be restricting your natural growth.

To help you get a handle on this, consider some of the following:

1. Are we providing effective ministry? Dr. Robert Schuller has stated the meaning of effective ministry like this: "Ministry is simply finding a hurt and healing it."

2. Do we really want to grow? It goes without saying that most of us have what we really want and what we are willing to pay the price to have.

3. Do we have a vision for growth? "Where there is no vision the people perish" (Proverbs 29:18). The way in which you are viewing your situation will very likely determine your actions.

4. Do you have leadership that is leading? Peter Wagner, in his book *Your Church Can Grow* (Glendale, CA: G/L Regal Publications, 1976), states that he would prefer to believe that the pastor is not the key to church growth, but his research has convinced him otherwise. This doesn't mean the pastor must do it all, but he must be the catalyst. I'm a pastor and I would like to reject this awesome responsibility, but all research proves that without a pastor with "church-growth eyes," it will not happen. It's God's plan.

5. Are you visible to your community? The people of your area must know where you are, who you really are, and what you can offer them.

6. Are you available? Your message and help must be accessible through a number of outlets.

7. Is your church alive? One of the most natural assumptions to make is that your church should grow. Jesus said, "I will build my church. . . ." Maybe you should take a hard look, much like a doctor would look at the health of your child if he/she stopped growing.

8. Have you set any goals? Define your purpose for being. Begin by writing a policy.

9. What are your priorities? If the world is to be evangelized by your church it must be made a priority! You cannot emphasize everything; therefore, when you set a priority you will let something else drop by the wayside, as not being essential to the top priority.

This is a process that will take some time and serious contemplation. But it's a very necessary step. In your evaluation, it will soon become apparent the direction that must be taken to continue or get involved in the changing of future direction. "For which of you, intending to build a tower, sitteth not down

first, and counteth the cost, whether he have sufficient to finish
it?'' (Luke 14:28). The future direction you take will be based
on the present evaluation. To get to your destination, you must
know where you are now and where and how you must go to
reach your future goal.

Do the People You Reach Also Leave?

Another aspect of this evaluation is to watch the flow of
people through your church. You may discover that you're
bringing them in through the front door only to have them leave
by the back door. It may seem as though you are doing a good
job because of the new faces, but you may not be showing any
measurable steady growth because of other factors that allow
your harvest to slip through your fingers. You may need to close
that back door by improving your effectiveness in training and
integrating those new people. Perhaps your "in-house" ministries need a drastic revision or improvement.

You might discover that you have no specific follow-up or
training program for new converts. Maybe you have no ministry
function that ensures that these new babes in Christ will be
loved and nourished. Many of our churches do quite well with
the delivery of newborn babes, but don't know what to do with
them after they have arrived. There are a myriad of suggestions
that could be implemented that will help you preserve the
harvest.

Evaluation may not appeal to you because of the difficulty in
getting a handle on the problem. But let me challenge you that
it must be carefully done if we are to be good stewards of the
message of hope that has been entrusted to us. If we do not
evaluate, we could well find ourselves like the man who flung
himself on his horse and rode off in all directions at the same
time.

6

Facilities and Staffing for Evangelism

A very unique and unusual method of evangelism has been practiced by a Rev. Jewel T. Pierce of Gadsden, Alabama, for the past 30 or more years. It seems that the good reverend has tossed some 30,000 whiskey bottles into the Coosa River which empties into the Gulf of Mexico. Each bottle contains a Bible message.

Many of the bottles have washed ashore along the river's winding way to sea, but many have not, as evidenced by the nearly 6,000 replies from 29 states and 8 foreign countries. Some have indicated their desire to trust Christ as their personal Saviour; some have called themselves backsliders who want to return to the church. One writer criticized the minister for wasting good bottles. The minister later discovered the critic was a bootlegger!

"Bottle" evangelism is an unusual way of sending out God's message, but it seems to have been one way of obeying Christ's commission. Our subject is still evangelism, but in a more specific way we will narrow our focus. And in no way am I recommending that each pastor and church begin a new type of evangelism called "bottle" outreach! I have only used this story as an attention getter to show you the many opportunities that we might have at our command.

I trust that you have taken your self-examination as suggested in the last chapter. Out of that evaluation should have come some kind of "theory for action." So now we turn to putting it into practice. To fail to act will lead to more despair and frustration. Here's a maxim that has an application at this point: "Impression without expression leads to depression."

Action Must Follow Evaluation

One of the most difficult things about a study like this is to move the average person and congregation from theory to practical action. A study on evangelism and the methods of evangelism must not be confused with evangelizing. For too long we have been great on listening, talking, planning, and then taking no action!

We are placing the premium upon action, but in no way does that detract from the previous step or the importance of sound theory. Faulty action can be caused by fuzzy thinking. These two go hand in glove and one should not be substituted for the other.

What Kind of Evangelism Will You Be Doing?

When we talk about staffing and facilities for evangelism, it might be well to preface that by taking a look at the kinds of evangelism you are preparing for.

Jesus practiced *spontaneous* and *planned* evangelism. An example of the spontaneous is the encounter with the Samaritan woman at the well. Weary from His travels, Jesus rested at Jacob's well. A woman approached Him, planning to draw water. He asked for a drink. This was a very normal and natural thing for an Eastern traveler to do. This woman with the scarlet past was fascinated by Christ's mention about the water of life, a drink that would satisfy. She became a Christian and, because of her enthusiasm and excitement, an entire village was converted. You can read the story in John 4:4-42. In fact, that chapter is worthy of intensive study in the methods of evangelism that Jesus used.

There are many more instances of spontaneous evangelism in the ministry of Christ. Consider the little man who climbed up a sycamore tree. Jesus spotted him and said: "Zaccheus, make haste, and come down; for today I must abide at thy house. . . . And Jesus said unto him, This day is salvation come to this house" (Luke 19:5, 9). Here was another convert! Jesus is one of the greatest examples of this evangelism we have called "spontaneous."

Just look at the fantastic possibilities in effectively carrying out this type of ministry. It's said that the average American comes in contact with at least 30 different people each day. These contacts include service personnel, checkout counters, employees at stores, fellow workers at the shop, casual contacts, school companions, and on and on. If your church has 100 members, theoretically, you could make 21,000 contacts for the gospel each week! Many of these contacts over a week's time would be the same people, but the constant contact with the same people ought to be more effective than the one-time meeting!

How do we go about staffing for this kind of evangelism? Staffing for spontaneous evangelism involves the enlistment of every person in your church. In reality, we are looking at a mass-training situation. What you presently are doing in your annual "Worker's Training" sessions is an excellent starting place. How about conducting a soul-winning clinic for your entire church? There are numerous methods that could be used, such as C. S. Lovett's "Soul-Winning Made Easy" or any of the training methods provided by Campus Crusade for Christ, with their "Four Spiritual Laws" approach. Or, you could go to your catalog from Gospel Publishing House and order one of the 19 different personal evangelism or witnessing tools or books. There is an abundance of materials available to you to teach soul winning to each believer in your church.

Think of the army that would be unleashed on our nation if every one of our members were committed to the spontaneous method of evangelism! To encourage the continuation of this kind of evangelism, make it a focus in each Sunday school class. Ask people to share their experiences. If you are made aware of a successful soul winner, have that person share his experience to encourage and challenge others. You can enlarge this focus by sermons or testimonies to the entire church. It is a process that must have a continual thrust. You will have what you emphasize.

What you will be doing is preparing your people to be "instant in season and out of season" and ready always to give a "reason for their faith." You must be challenged with the limitless possibilities that spontaneous evangelism will open up for each Christian. Be encouraged to expect opportunities for witnessing in every human encounter and be ready to respond.

Evangelism becomes an exciting process that is a natural part of life.

Planned Evangelism

Jesus was also involved in planned evangelism. He sent out the Seventy on a planned missionary adventure into every town and village (Luke 10:2). He gave them explicit instructions on how they were to act, what they were not to do, what they should do in the event of rejection, and how they were to be supported. He prepared them for all the potential situations they would face. (Read the narrative from Luke 10:1-24.)

A church that hopes to reach every unsaved person in the community cannot rely only on spontaneous evangelism to get the job done. Our Lord said that He came to "seek and to save the lost" (Luke 19:10, RSV). The process of seeking will be the planned evangelism that each congregation must engage in. The New Testament Church set the tone as they went "house to house" (Acts 20:20, 21).

Many people will be lost unless they are actively sought out. Many Christians are reluctant to get involved in this kind of an activity because of the fear of rejection or for fear that they will invade another's privacy. Remember that there are millions of desperate, lonely people in our world who would welcome your extended hand of friendship and your message of hope!

Staffing Begins With a Basic Organization

Staffing for evangelism should start with a basic simplified structure. Organization will allow the job to be done in a systematic manner. Organize a "committee on evangelism" to begin pulling the task together, to break it down into immediate and long-range goals, to delegate the tasks, and to define responsibilities and correlate the entire task.

Select people with vision and people with organizational ability. Administrators form the link between the "dream" and the steps that have to be taken to move that mountain. How will you plan to reach your community? Will you have a door-to-door survey? Would your town lend itself to a systematic telephone canvass? How will you gather the materials needed?

Will you be using the mass media for your *blitz?* Will it be planned as an ongoing program or will it take place in a month? Let the definition flow out from your committee. It may be composed of an already existing church board, a Sunday school staff, a professional staff, or an appointed committee of people with a genuine interest in this ministry.

The organizational phase will be followed by the recruiting drive. At this point, we are only talking about evangelism; we haven't done any of it yet. This is a particularly critical time, for now, all this theory must become action. The body must now make it happen, and this is a time that should be open to all who are a part of your church. Your response will be more enthusiastic when people know they will be trained and given assignments with authority to perform in their job. There are people who are eager to invest their time, talent, and treasure in reaching the lost! You will need people to organize the effort, some to do the actual contacting, and others to conserve the harvest. This is not to say that one job is greater than any other, but that all are necessary to have an effective harvest.

Make a check on your motives for evangelism. If you are seeking to grow the biggest church in town or extend the influence of your institution so you can brag about "how we did it," the lost you seek will be totally unimpressed and unresponsive, because your motives will show through. The lost must be sought for their own sakes by those who have the love of Christ.

I have purposely not spoken in specifics for fear of excluding you and possibly your church or your situation. Each situation is unique and the mix of ministry for outreach that works best in your area is your responsibility. Staffing is people and people are always more important than facilities. But, before we leave this area of staffing, be assured that there are a myriad of techniques to effective evangelism that other churches have used successfully in their particular situations. I also believe that the Holy Spirit, who is the Person of infinite variety, will guide you and direct you in totally new approaches that no one else has yet used! Be creative! What church can expect significant growth without adequate preparation and follow-through? It's a matter of planning and working your plan.

Look at Facilities

Now, let's shift gears to look at facilities for evangelism. Can facilities minister to people? There are three basics that are part of the process in a Sunday school setting: the teacher, who is always the most important; the curriculum, which is the content of the material being taught; and the room itself or the setting. The facility is not the most important; in fact, it may be the least important, but it is a factor you must consider. Some of you may be thinking: "Our church building is in such bad shape that it won't work!" or, "We need a new building so bad that until it happens, it's just no use for us to make an effort at evangelism!" Any facility can be improved!

According to God's Word, the care and feeding of a facility is important. The care we give to our buildings is a testimony about our love for God. Solomon had led the people of Israel in building a beautiful temple for God's glory. However, we find in 2 Chronicles 28, 29, 33, and 34, that the people of Israel had lost their love for their God and, as a result, their temple had deteriorated. Josiah and Hezekiah were two kings who repaired the temple and restored it from its neglected condition to its former beauty.

Look at your church and your classroom or rooms. Would you like to spend 2 hours there next Sunday if you didn't have to? Would it be a pleasant place to spend an hour if no one else was there with you?

Your facility and its condition are one of the boldest and loudest statements you are making to your community! There are some things that are tough to change, such as the size of a room, the placement of windows, or the slant of the floor. But there are other immediate concerns that should mark every church facility. Run down this checklist with me:

1. Is the room/church clean? There is a story about a little boy who was walking down the halls of his church with his mother. As they walked, the boy turned to his mother and said, "Mommy, these people don't love Jesus do they?" The mother, who was quite surprised, asked why he felt that way. "Because their windows are dirty!" I can't vouch for the truth of that story, but the principle still hold. You've heard it from childhood up: "Cleanliness is next to godliness."

2. Are things in good repair? There is nothing that so depresses children and adults as to see something that is broken. Remove any broken fixtures or furniture until repairs can be made.

3. In what condition is the paint? Color can easily set the mood for your church or classroom. Certain colors have an effect on people. Some colors stimulate while others tend to make a person drowsy. Paint is relatively inexpensive and any room in drab condition can be improved through a wise selection of paint.

4. Do you have enough light? Lighting that is adequate is a must. The minimum standard should call for at least 35 foot-candles of reflected light at the tabletop level. If you think you need help with this, contact your local light company and you will discover that they can be very helpful in determining your lighting needs.

5. Have you looked at the floor covering lately? Is the carpeting in good repair, with no holes showing? With carpet on a floor you could remove all the furniture and sit your children on the floor, expanding the size capability of your class.

6. How about the ventilation? Keep your class and church in the comfort range with heating and cooling that is sufficient.

7. Have you added a decorative touch? How about curtains at the windows, suitable paintings or pictures on the walls, bulletin boards in good repair, etc.? You will find that these little touches can add so much in the way of pride for a facility.

Yes, facilities for evangelism are important. They, too, must be part of your complete message to the unreached. Your building and your care of it are interpreted by the world as your expression of the importance of the God you serve.

If You Plan to Build . . .

Perhaps a word or two would be in order if you are planning a new facility. If we believe in the concept that just as we shape our environment (buildings), so our environment will have an effect in shaping us, then any building or shaping of buildings must be done with care.

Get some professional guidance. For instance, do you know that in planning for preschool children (birth to kindergarten) that a minimum of 35 square feet per child is needed to allow for the best teaching/learning situation? Are you also aware that a minimum of 9 to 12 square feet is the recommended space per adult? With such information a new facility can be planned that is usable to the greatest extent in helping your evangelism efforts.(Here is a recommended book: *Focus: Building for Christian Education*, by Mildred C. Widber and Scott Turner Ritenour [Princeton, NJ: Pilgrim Press]. In it you will find data, charts, forms, and excellent suggestions.)

The celebration of a new building is a unique and wonderful experience. It can be a pilgrimage into new and greater outreach. There are those critics today who question any church's need for a building for any purpose in the face of the world's needs, or they argue that the New Testament Church was largely a "house" church. But until such time as new forms of ministry and witness are available to us, a church building is still the most functional tool we have.

Where and how would young children be nurtured in the Christian faith and life if it were not for a church building? Where would adults and youth be challenged to best serve and evangelize their world? How would your church function without a facility?

Facilities and staffing are tools with which to reach, teach, and mature the unreached. Often we can be so caught up in the development and maintenance of the tools that we forget the main task ahead of us. Staffing and facilities? Absolutely *yes!* But keep them within the boundaries of balance. They are not the ends in themselves but are some of the means that help us to reach the lost. Reaching the lost is a priority that must not be lost in mechanics or buildings! Jesus commanded us to go into all the world to reach the lost—not buildings or monuments.

7

Training Each Person for Evangelism

Evangelism can be taught! Evangelism should be as natural as breathing for every person in the church! Evangelism is the very purpose for our existence as a church. To know this by theory or by a challenge is not enough in itself; Biblical principles must be put into action.

If evangelism that reaches this world is to take place in our day, each local church must be able to translate the concepts into an actual working program. There is a real scarcity of working models for the local church to pattern itself after. Many of the cults have outdone the true church of Jesus Christ in their ability to train and motivate their people for their ministry.

It's our purpose in this chapter to propose a model from which a church can effectively implement evangelism through the preparation of each person. We'll talk in terms of principles that can be applied to each local situation. This involves the following steps.

Lay a Solid Foundation of Principles

There must be an awareness that God is calling His people to greatness and evangelism. If people will understand and have a vision of the "big picture" they will respond and want to get involved in the harvest.

Church growth and evangelism are as old as the Bible and as new as today! You can see the beginnings of this principle in God's dealings with Abraham. God told Abraham: "In thee shall all families of the earth be blessed" (Genesis 12:3). God calls people to follow Him and, as they do, He pours His blessings into their lives; then He calls them to be a blessing to others. God will bless and reach this world with His message through people. You can trace this principle through the entire history of God's people from Abraham through the Early Church on down to our present day!

The Bible is alive and bubbling over with the theme of growth and outreaching. In our training of each person there must be an awareness that this is the overriding theme of God's Word and plan. It can be seen in God's single purpose in sending Jesus Christ to this earth: "For the Son of man is come to seek and to save that which was lost" (Luke 19:10). There can be no argument as to the singleness of purpose in that verse! "The Lord is . . . long-suffering to us-ward, not willing that any should perish, but that all should come to repentance" (2 Peter 3:9).

In establishing and laying the purpose for evangelism, it must be apparent that the commission is very clear and positively stated. It is not something that has been hatched by a Sunday school teacher, a pastor, or a superintendent. It is the very heart cry of God!

> As Moses lifted up the serpent in the wilderness, even so must the Son of man be lifted up: that whosoever believeth in him should not perish, but have eternal life (John 3:14, 15).

It is not the idea of any particular person; it is the purpose of God for our day! God, "who will have all men to be saved" (1 Timothy 2:4), is the One who is giving the commission to each person. There is no higher purpose stated in God's Word than the imperative of evangelism, and this must be made perfectly clear to each person who is a worker in the harvest.

GOD BUILDS HIS CHURCH THROUGH PEOPLE

It must also be firmly established that *each* person is a participant in the harvest. There can be no unemployment in the whitened fields of harvest in this world. The message demands that there must be a messenger, the harvest field makes it clear that there must be a harvester, and the mandate demands a follow-through. God's plan and purpose is clear and easy to grasp. The problem that most of us face is making a practical application of this to our life-style. God has always worked in and through people; in fact, He has limited himself to finite people.

This need for a messenger is clearly stated by the apostle Paul in Romans 10:14, as he challenges: "How then shall they call on him . . . ? And how shall they believe in him . . . ? And how shall they hear without a preacher?" When most of us hit the word *preacher*, we automatically excuse ourselves. We are not preachers, therefore the job must be done by our "preacher." The *New English Bible* translates it like this: " . . . without *someone* to spread the news?" The original Greek speaks in terms of a proclamation of the gospel and in no way is it used as we would use the term *preacher* today. When Paul wrote this, there were no professional preachers; everyone in the church was considered a messenger.

Read again Acts 8:4: "Therefore they that were scattered abroad went every where preaching the word." Note the context and you will discover that the "they" who "went everywhere preaching the word" were the church, which was composed of lay people. If we leave this task to our preachers, it will never get done because it is too large. The messenger must be each and every person who is part of the Kingdom fellowship.

After the resurrection of Jesus Christ there was fear among the disciples. Apparently they went into hiding because they feared being the next ones to be crucified. It must have been a very pessimistic gathering behind closed doors as they plotted future strategy. Could they have been speculating on how they would now return to a normal life-style? Were they wondering how they could have been so taken in by a person and a story?

We don't know. But this we do know: "Jesus [came] and stood in the midst" (John 20:19). He offered peace to them. Then He showed them His hands and side so there could be no doubt that it was Him. And the disciples reacted with joy! Then, lest there be any mistakes about their future and their place in His ministry, He stated: "As my Father hath sent me, even so send I you" (John 20:21). They were recommissioned and put back into service. He made a course correction that put aside any doubts about their future ministry. They were to follow through and complete the commission of the Father to the Son; it now passed from the Son to the Church. That's right, you and I are the Church!

In laying these foundational principles there must be an urgency. Each person must grasp the heartthrob of Jesus Christ. There can be no question about who the "sent one" is to be.

THE HOLY SPIRIT WILL ENABLE

We take that commissioning another step when we discover that a power to enable the harvest to take place is found in Acts 1:7, 8:

> He [Jesus] said unto them, It is not for you to know the times or the seasons, which the Father hath put in his own power. But ye shall receive power, after that the Holy Ghost is come upon you: and *ye shall be witnesses unto me* both in Jerusalem, and in all Judea, and in Samaria, and unto the uttermost part of the earth.

There is no way we can escape the implications of that command! It's even more emphatic than the famous recruiting poster of World War II that had Uncle Sam pointing his finger at the viewer and saying, "I need you!"

"You shall be witnesses unto me . . . " cannot be stated more emphatically in the original Greek. There is a must, an urgency, about that statement. It goes without saying that this is one of the most important reasons for the infilling of the Holy Spirit.

Christ's concern for building His church is a well-established principle as well as a statement as to the people who will be the instruments through which this process will continue. Let's look again at Matthew 28:19, 20 from Phillips' translation:

> You, then, are to go and make disciples of all the nations and baptize them in the name of the Father and of the Son and of the Holy Spirit. Teach them to observe all that I have commanded you and, remember, I am with you always, even to the end of the world.

If you read the context of the previous verses (Matthew 28:16-18), you will discover that this commission was given to the disciples; and, by inference, if you are a disciple or follower of Jesus Christ, the commission has been given to you— to you in big cities, to you in little towns, to you who are educated, to you who are reading this book right now, and to me!

GOD WILL BLESS HIS MINISTRY

Here's another principle that is foundational to understanding the harvest: the Lord did bless and will bless this pattern of ministry in the Early Church and in His church today. It really happened, and God will bless any church or group of people or any individual who is committed to the harvest. Each of us must know that when we obey God, obedience is blessed with results and growth! You can verify this by looking into the Book of "The Acts of the Apostles." Perhaps we should rename it "The Acts of the Church With the Confirmation of the Holy Spirit."

It starts in Acts 1:15: "And in those days Peter stood up in the midst of the disciples, and said, (the number of names together were about a hundred and twenty,). . . ." Numbers and growth were important. They were so important to the Holy Spirit that great care was used in recording them for us. Acts 2:41 tells us: "And the same day there were added unto them about three thousand souls." There's more growth! And on to 2:47: "And the Lord added to the church daily such as should be saved." That infant church was only a few days old, but they numbered at least 3,120! And that number was growing on a daily basis. That's pretty good church growth! Evangelism was effective, and it happened through those commissioned disciples and then through their followers!

It didn't stop there! We can follow the progress of explosive growth to Acts 4:4: "Howbeit many of them which heard the word believed; and the number of the men was about five thousand." How many more of the women and children became Christians because of those men? Continue to Acts 5:14: "And believers were the more added to the Lord, multitudes both of men and women."

Then, God's arithmetic changed from addition to multiplication in Acts 6:1: "And in those days, when the number of the disciples was multiplied. . . ." Please take note that all the new Christians were called "disciples." The Greek word is *mathetes*, which means "one who professes to have learned certain principles from another."

Look at Acts 6:7: "And the word of God increased; and the number of the disciples multiplied in Jerusalem *greatly;* and a great company of the priests were obedient to the faith." Who increased the spreading of the Word? The disciples! Even the very new disciples! It's obvious that the Lord blessed the church that carried out the commission to evangelize. There was spectacular as well as consistent growth.

It wasn't only the Jerusalem church that grew, take a look at Acts 9:31: "Then had the churches rest throughout all Judea and Galilee and Samaria, and were edified; and walking in the fear of the Lord, and in the comfort of the Holy Ghost, *were multiplied.*" Now it seems that a number of new churches appeared and were multiplied in size and number of new congregations. This ingathering of the lost spread to areas beyond the borders of Israel, as indicated in Acts 11:19-21 with the mention of more growth in Phoenicia, Cyprus, Cyrene, and Antioch: "And the hand of the Lord was with them: and a great number believed, and turned unto the Lord."

Could it happen elsewhere? Follow the journey of Paul to the east and north in Acts 16:5: "And so were the churches established in the faith, and increased in number daily." Here is the spread of the gospel among the Greeks in Derbe and Lystra. It happened again! And it was a "daily" occurrence, not just on Sundays only.

God will bless and wants to bless the individual and the church that involve themselves personally in the harvest! It's a principle that God will always honor. If the foundational principles are to be a part of each Christian's experience, they must be taught in every Sunday school class to every student!

Develop a Positive Identity

For too long, many of our lay people have felt not needed or unnecessary in the harvest field. Many of our students have an inferiority complex and there may be many reasons for this. Could it be that we have not emphasized the importance of the individual Christian? Are we to blame because we have encouraged the "superstar" type of Christian as the only one whom God can use as a witness? We don't have the time to develop or to answer the reasons for such thinking, other than to note it as a possible problem that needs some serious rethinking on our part.

We are in the harvest together! The leadership in a church is the key to effecting changes in attitudes. People must hear leaders say and practice the fact that we, all of us, are playing on the same team. The pastor is the coach, but he can't do the playing all by himself. How about a study to show each person that the backbone of God's redemptive plan throughout history has been to use people just like us to be God's hand reaching out to the lost? Each person is a minister!

I'm really saying that we need to make the transition, in each person's life, from the role of being a spectator to an active role in the life and mission of the Church. Paul said some very helpful things to the church at Corinth: "I . . . planted, Apollos watered; but God gave the increase" (1 Corinthians 3:6). This shows the interaction of God with man, as well as man and man.

When your church grows, it will be because God has given an increase to the planting, watering, and nurturing of some person—perhaps you! God has placed the ministries of evangelizing in the hands of people. Without people to carry out the commands of the Great Commission, God will have nothing to bless or increase!

There is no such thing as an unimportant person in the harvest field! This is a dynamic essential in the transition of the student from spectator status to that of being an active participant. A properly focused study will build the believer's self-image. We are part of the greatest and most fantastic plan ever devised. We are more than "just" church members, we are part of God's victorious army! We are God's agents of redemption! We can't produce redemption, only God can, but His cleansing of the sinful soul will not happen until another person is the agent of that change.

There can be ongoing teaching as well as a formal set time of instruction. It should be incorporated into the teaching and preaching of every church. It can best be implemented through an educational program in concert with the pulpit to build this identity. This need is one of identification of a "lay minister" concept. You will know you have been successful when it is believed to the point where it is translated into action! The action you will be looking for is evangelism on the part of each person in your church, as well as the growth of your church.

James, the brother of our Lord, illustrates this principle from the life of Elijah. His implication is that if Elijah is like us in our humanness, we can be like him in his praying: "Elijah was a man subject to like passions as we are, and he prayed earnestly that it might not rain. . . . And he prayed again . . ." (James 5:17, 18). Most of us picture Elijah under the juniper tree asking to die. When God paints word pictures of His people in the Word, He usually paints them "wart" and all, to show us that common people are the ones used in His kingdom.

> For ye see your calling, brethren, how that not many wise men after the flesh, not many mighty, not many noble, are called: but God hath chosen the foolish [common or not considered great] things of the world to confound the wise; and God hath chosen the weak [insignificant] things of the world to confound the things which are mighty (1 Corinthians 1:26, 27).

God takes people where they are and makes them into effective instruments of righteousness. The process still goes on today. We must convey to each person the imperative for everyone to be part of the harvest process. I know this is a theme that has been used before in this book, but it bears repeating. It is one of the major keys to breaking the logjam of talent lying dormant in His church.

God cannot bless inaction or complacency. The Word has given us illustrations to show us that God can and will bless any person or people who will initiate action on His behalf. Nothing happens until there is a human vessel to make it happen. Humans can't bless their own efforts, only God can. And by the same token, God won't do anything that has been left for the Church to do, but He will bless with growth each effort made by His church, by His people. To convey this reality until it becomes action, will take every bit of ingenuity and love you have as a leader/teacher. It is a step that must be taken before effective soul winning takes place.

Use the Same Pattern Christ Did

Jesus believed in and used a method that was based on the principle that a small group of well-prepared and trained disciples could permeate and reach a much larger group. This would happen in much the same way that a little bit of yeast in bread dough influences (or leavens) the whole loaf (Luke 13:21). Jesus didn't only teach this, He put it into practice in His own training of the Twelve. He invested himself in a relationship that had purpose. He was able, in about 3 short years, to train them by indelibly stamping their lives for ministry in a way that they would not forget.

This pattern is important for the church today that is involved in equipping each person for harvesting. The Sunday school setting can be an ideal small-group situation in which the very same principles of training can be used. In this manner, we can prepare a cluster of people over a continuing period of time. Normal classroom settings can be adapted, with a few changes, to become an intensive training center for evangelism. This could be done in each class as an ongoing churchwide emphasis for a specified period, or it could happen in a single class created for this purpose.

Teaching should be followed by weekly study, interaction, and practical application. I would suggest that a discipleship class last for at least 1 year to really be effective in conveying the concepts. If you have an elective program, this vehicle could be used very effectively here. People could be recruited or invited to be part of an extended discipleship training program.

Many of our churches are moving into a home fellowship ministry. This is also an ideal setting for the teaching of discipleship based on the pattern we take from the Master.

Jesus Christ taught the lesson by laying foundational principles. He told them what He expected of them and how they were to do it. The classic pattern is seen in the sending of the Seventy. They returned rejoicing to tell Him of their successes, which in turn He followed up with another lesson. It was a cycle He used: select them, associate with them, teach them, demonstrate for them, delegate the responsibility, supervise their activity, and watch them in reproduction. The very same principles will also work in today's world.

If you use the Sunday school, the pastor could teach the teachers who, in turn, will teach the students. Or, if you use the structure of the home fellowship groups, again the pastor or another designated person could meet with the leaders to teach them, and they in turn could convey the truth to each participant.

An important aspect is to begin with people who are willing to stay with the program through its cycle of completion. Let's say you choose to make this an elective. You will need to have the participants remain with it for the duration of time by their own commitment. It's very difficult to teach and implement a discipleship program if you have a continuous turnover in class members. Continuity is needed to do a thorough job of conveying the principles. After the training is completed with the first group, please make plans to have this small group of committed people get involved in another training program in which they will be the leaders. In this way, the multiplication effect of the "pyramid principle" will be working for you.

Develop Your Own Ongoing Training Center

Evangelism is too important to make one stab at it and then let it drop. It must be a continuing emphasis. The dynamics of your own lay ministry must be part of the life of your congregation before a training center will be effective.

Begin by determining the areas of needed ministry in the life of your church and community. One of the primary needs will be to train lay people as evangelists to share Christ with people who are unchurched. That's the basic: training to reach the lost. This is foundational training that every person should have in your church. Perhaps you could then move into a telephone counseling ministry and train your folk for this phase.

To help you focus on potential ministries, answer this question: "What is Christ asking us as a church to do to reach our community?" The answer will give you direction in developing your own ongoing training programs. If you cannot decide your mission in the light of God's Word and the needs of your community, you will likely not be a growing church. It is the church that has its purpose in sharp focus and can motivate its people to carry out that mission that will experience growth. It is the church with the vision in mind that will be able to turn the lay person to move for God. You have people in your church who are waiting to be challenged. These are the people who will respond in a fashion that translates into action . . . and soon they will set off a chain reaction.

Stop a moment for a word of encouragement. Your program doesn't need to be elaborate or only something that can be done in a large church. The smallest church can move in this direction. Didn't Jesus start by selecting only 12? Any training you set up must be functional. There are certain principles that apply to all of us, but the specifics are individualized. Your church will function at its best when it helps its own body of believers. The Biblical picture of the church is like that of a human body, and we have long ago discovered that there are no unnecessary parts. At least most of us are not ready to give any of them away!

Even the Insignificant Is Important

Many of us tend to think in terms that shrink our importance and therefore we think we can't be effective. I had an uncle, now deceased, who lost the little finger on his right hand in a woodcutting accident. As a boy I was fascinated with that hand that had no little finger.

One day when he was visiting in our home, I asked, "Uncle Olaf, do you miss your little finger?" He gave me one of those special looks he always seemed to have for inquisitive boys, and said, "Yes . . . a little finger doesn't seem to be very much. But did you know that when you close your hand to pick something up, it forms the bottom and closes it so the object you pick up doesn't slip on through?" Then he illustrated by picking up a glass. He went on to say that at first he had dropped lots of full glasses of milk until he learned to compensate for this loss.

So it is in the spiritual Body. Paul tells us there are no unimportant parts in the Body: "Those members of the body, which seem to be more feeble, are necessary" (1 Corinthians 12:22). Discipleship training is the means of equipping each believer with the necessary tools for the task. It must be relevant and give meaning to the Christian experience.

Keep one aspect in mind (it's something the academic community has discovered). Just because you have excellent courses or the right kind of educational process or the best teachers, together these will not guarantee success or an actual living out of the materials taught. A positive sense of purpose and urgency will overcome this. People who make progress in the training experience are the same ones who are also involved directly in some phase of Christ's mission. Let's help people to move beyond theory to actual life practice.

The growth numerically and spiritually you experience in your church will be largely determined by your obedience to Christ's Great Commission. This is one of the highest callings of the church: to train each person who is part of that specific body of believers. Don't you think it's about time we took the mission seriously and got on with the training?

In the pioneer church my father pastored in Mansfield, Ohio, during the early 1940s, a lady came and gave her life to Christ. The next service she brought along her 5-year-old daughter. Mother and daughter attended church on a regular basis. Only on rare occasions would the husband attend. He was a huge man who worked in a local foundry. He'd been quite a football player, too. This man prided himself on the fact that no preacher or evangelist could get to him. If he came to a preaching service, he'd fold his arms in defiance of the messenger.

One day, their little girl fell sick. The parents were worried because she didn't respond to any of their home remedies, so they took her to the doctor for help. Her illness was diagnosed as acute leukemia with no hope for survival or recovery. She was sent home to be cared for until her condition became so bad that she had to be hospitalized.

Life changed drastically for that little family. It seemed that her condition worsened rapidly and soon she was confined to complete bed rest. The very first stop that devoted father would make on coming home from work was her bedside. It was obvious to the father and mother that she wouldn't be with them much longer.

On one particular day, the dad arrived home and went directly into that little convalescent room and knelt at her bedside, so he could look her right in the eye. She had lost so much weight that now bones could be seen where once there had been the plumpness of childhood, her eyes were a bit sunken, but they still sparkled as she looked at her daddy.

"Daddy," she said, "I know that I'm going to die and go to be with Jesus. And, Daddy," she continued, gasping for each breath in the struggle to talk, "my Sunday school teacher told me when I get to heaven Jesus will give me a crown and I will have a star in my crown for each person who I lead to Christ."

She lifted her head off the pillow to get a better look at her daddy, as she reached for him with those tiny hands and went on, "Daddy, I don't have any stars in my crown because I haven't led anybody to accept Jesus."

By this time that big old dad had tears trickling down his face as she reached for his neck to pull him closer. She looked right into his eyes and asked, "Daddy, will you give your heart to Jesus so that I can have a star in my crown when I get to heaven?"

The mother had been standing in the doorway and had seen the nodding of his head and heard his halting reply, "Yes . . . honey, I will." The mother came and knelt beside that man and they all prayed together in a glorious time.

It was just a day or two later that she went into a coma and then on to heaven. After the funeral, at the very next church service, both her mother and father were there. Testimonies were called for and this father was the first person on his feet. He said, "Would you please let me say this?" Without waiting for any response, he went on, "I gave my heart to Jesus Christ because my little girl asked me to." He paused as the tears started flowing, then he continued, "There was no other person in this world who could have touched me but my little girl. I'm so glad she went to a church like this and had a Sunday school teacher who was concerned about a little girl who, in turn, was concerned about me."

Every Christian can be a participant in this harvest! There are people out there that only you are able to reach for Christ. Training and encouraging your students will allow them the joy of participating in the reaping of the lost.

8

The Sunday School as a Tool of Evangelism

The time has come for us to take another exciting look at one of the greatest tools for evangelism that has been placed in our hands—the *Sunday school!* Look at it through a new dimension—growth! Really see it with a new understanding—the purpose for which we have been called!

Sunday schools have played an important role in the ministry of our churches in the past, and we can only anticipate an increased role in the future. Our past is a rich heritage that has been led forward by our Christian education through Sunday schools, and we project that the future is bright for growth.

A Short Look at the History of the Sunday School

The Sunday school is a bit over 200 years old, having not long ago celebrated the anniversary of its founding by Robert Raikes (1780-1980). It started in "Sooty Alley" of Gloucester, England, and later John Wesley adopted the Sunday school as "one of the noblest instruments to be seen in Europe for some centuries." It's not a Biblical institution as some have thought, but it is based on Biblical principles.

It came to America and most church organizations took it in hand about 1827, and through the remainder of the 19th century it grew in fertile ground. During the 20th century it continued to flourish at a record pace. Growth seemed to happen with almost no effort. From the very beginnings of the Assemblies of God, our Sunday schools have pretty well set the pace for the growth we have experienced.

All is not completely well in the Sunday school, however. As we moved into the 1960's and 1970's, the patterns of growth seemed to change. First it was plateaus that were reached; to be followed by declines, with some of the mainline denominations showing as much as a 45 percent decline over the last decade. There are 42 major Protestant denominations in America and of that number, only 12 have shown any measurable growth during the last year of complete statistics (1979). Fortunately, the Assemblies of God was among those showing growth.

Consider that in the past decade, the Assemblies of God has had a church membership growth of 54 percent and during the same period, a Sunday school growth of 23 percent. Our churches are growing faster in church membership than we are growing in Sunday school attendance. Why? There was a time when we had tremendous "Sunday school conventions" with thousands in attendance and all kinds of enthusiasm over slogans and Sunday school methods. We grew as we emphasized campaigns of "every-member-bring-one." We are and have been a revival movement! Forward we went, as we pushed evangelism in the Sunday school.

Today, there is an alarming trend away from the emphasis on quality Christian education in some areas. The Sunday school is being replaced by a midweek school or no school at all. To take its place there is an expanded worship experience, which is good, too. But this is an emphasis that should be reversed because quality Christian education is a foundation. On the other hand, we have some of the fastest growing schools our Movement has ever seen! There is hope for today's Sunday school!

We need to be reaching, enlisting, winning, and discipling people into our fellowships. Sunday school is still one of the most vital ways in which this can be made to happen. Some schools are fading into nothingness, while others are booming with vitality. Why? What makes one school grow while another stagnates? Is it the quality of teaching that makes the difference? Do you have to have a fleet of buses in order to grow? Must you have one fantastic contest after another? Can growing schools only be found in urban areas? Is there a key?

The Major Factor of Growing Schools

Win Arn of the "Institute for American Church Growth"

(Pasadena, California) has stated that the major difference between growing schools and nongrowing schools can be shown in a single concept—*purpose!* His research in church growth indicates that the "purpose for being" is nearly always different in growing and declining churches.

Schools on the decline are the ones that have made their major purpose for being a ministry that is exclusive to their own. Don't get me wrong, we must take care of our own, but the facts show that schools on a plateau or decline have made "maintenance of status quo" the major focus. It is sort of like the man who prayed in this fashion, "Lord, bless me and mine and no more!"

When the focus is placed within, people are encouraged to participate because of what it will do for "me." The church then becomes a refugee camp for believers. Everything is done for the personal welfare and concerns of that group. Here is where you can hear that infamous quote as rationalization: "We may not be growing, but do we ever have spiritual believers!" To give strength to this thinking, there is a current philosophy that growth will naturally result from personal growth and development. Education that is self-centered will not motivate your people toward outreach. This mind-set has a tendency to keep us within our "monastery" or "fortress," sealed off from the real world. It's easy, then, to think: "We are the good guys and they are the big bad world!"

Having an orientation that is only "nurturing" in emphasis is to commit the error of making Sunday school an end in itself. Jesus Christ has commanded the Church to reach out, to carry ministry to others who have needs. If your church is plateauing or declining in attendance, check your priorities! Look carefully at materials, facilities, teacher training, and teachers—do they reflect Christ's priority of extending?

Growing Schools Exist to Reach Out

Growing churches exist to carry out Christ's Great Commission! They are in the business of soul winning, loving, reaching, training, and equipping each person for ministry to this desperate world. With a balance, there will still be a concern for the maturation of the existing members, but this becomes part of the process and not the end.

For your church to move to such a stance for existence, you need to rethink your concept of "Christian education." In reality, it should be "missionary education" by actual practice. It is as we participate in Christ's mission that we have reason to exist. His purpose, as stated in 1 Timothy 2:4, is to "have all men to be saved, and to come unto the knowledge of the truth."

Schools that look outward, that have the focus of evangelism, see these two functions as compatible. Training and evangelism are the two goals that really are one. Let's go so far as to say that "Christian education" is not really Christian until it is also evangelistic! The most spiritual thing you can do is to lead another person to Jesus Christ. Is there any other basis on which to justify our existence?

Think what would happen if every teacher and each class existed for the top priority of reaching and teaching people! Growth! Evangelism! Outreach! The results will always be the same: " . . . and God gave the increase"!

This is not saying that for you to turn your school into an evangelistic thrust you will have to abandon spiritual nurture. Reach and teach at the same time. Take a page from Christ's own methods. He spent lots of time training His disciples, but this was the means to the end of reaching a Christless world for Christ. Read the "Acts of the Apostles" and see for yourself the ways in which the students of Christ built the Church. When your major goal is making disciples, you are well aware that quality education is the supporting foundation. They are both necessary.

The starting point in using your Sunday school as an evangelistic tool is to set priorities: check your purpose for existence and decide whether you will be an inward- or outward-directed school, Christ-honoring or dishonoring, obedient to the Great Commission or disobedient. Your Sunday school can make the major contribution to the growth of your church. It is a unique and beautiful arm of the church. Your Sunday school can do things that no other organization of your church can do.

Let's look at some of the principles for evangelism in and through your Sunday school:

THE SUNDAY SCHOOL IS AN EVANGELISTIC OUTREACH

How did you become part of your local church? The chances are that about 80 percent or even more of you did so because you had a relative or friend that already was a member! There are a number of surveys showing the same results. Some say 70 percent, while others say as high as 90 percent, of all new people who are attending a particular church do so because of a bridge of friendship that has already been established. Think of the possibilities that exist in your church to reach a vast number of people. Surely all of us have friends, neighbors, and relatives that we have not invited to be part of the family of God.

That brings us to the suggestion that your church should have a training session or sessions as part of your programming to teach people how to reach relatives and acquaintances. How about designating an entire quarter of your year to evangelism training? Try a planned curriculum on soul-winning evangelism. Yes, even down to the little people in your school. There are many benefits that would be derived; entire families would be studying the same material and would reinforce each other. It would be the major thrust of your entire church for a 13-week period.

The pulpit should also be used to encourage and supplement this training. Prepare family devotions about this subject. Let it become a complete saturation process. Feature people who are having results in their personal witnessing through personal testimony. The possibilities are totally unlimited.

THE SUNDAY SCHOOL PROVIDES UNIQUE FELLOWSHIP OPPORTUNITIES

Here is a structure ready-made for developing personal relationships. Fellowship has been defined as "two fellows in the same ship." Too often we have a misconception of what fellowship is in the church. We think that if we come to church and look at the back of someone's head, shake a hand or two, and listen to the sermon, we have fellowshipped. Not so.

Fellowship, among other things, is building relationships that help and encourage each other. The Bible uses the phrase "one another" at least 31 times, with many different applications. Some specific applications are: "Love one another,"

"edify one another," "be devoted one to another," "admonish
one another," "be like-minded one to another," "comfort one
another," and so on. You can hardly do that while sitting in a
pew! But you can do some or most of these things in a small-
group situation with caring, loving people. These "one
another" actions can be done on a continuing basis from week
to week through the structure of a Sunday school class.

The relationships we have with people will reflect our relationship with God the Father:

> If a man [or woman] say, I love God, and hateth his [her]
> brother, he [she] is a liar: for he [she] that loveth not his
> [her] brother whom he [she] hath seen, how can he [she]
> love God whom he [she] hath not seen? (1 John 4:20).

Koinonia relationships are necessary in every church. These
can be a direct result of what happens each Sunday as people
have the opportunity of building these ties with each other.
Here is an opportunity for ministry to each other as well as
reaching beyond the confines of the class. Perhaps you may
have to restructure your classroom time to allow this to happen.
At this point, you can put to use one of the major keys to future
church growth. Strong personal bonds that are loving and caring will enhance your entire church. People want to be part of
us when they see Jesus expressed in our people-to-people
contacts. It's a strong attraction to lonely people. It will greatly
help in incorporating new people into the life of the church.

There will be a carry-over from the classroom to the real-life
world. You'll find people sharing together outside of the
church. They'll be working together, visiting the sick ones in
the hospital, stopping by with a sack of groceries for someone in
need, and encouraging one another. God has not called any of
us to be the "lone Christian." The body of Christ was intended
to be complete with the contributions each part of the Body
makes to the other. Fellowship makes the church the church.

THE SUNDAY SCHOOL PROVIDES THE BEST OPPORTUNITY TO IMPART
BIBLICAL KNOWLEDGE

People are crying out for answers to life's perplexities. God has an answer for the complexities of life. Biblical knowledge is at an all-time low. The *Christianity Today* Gallup Poll referred to earlier shows us that about 53 percent of the American population claim a life-changing religious experience. Almost half, 69 million people age 18 and over, of the 53 percent are hoping to go to heaven only because of their personal faith in Jesus Christ. And more than 100 million adults are members of a church or synagogue.

"Great!" you say. But fewer than 3 in 10 people can correctly identify, "Ye must be born again," as the words of Jesus; fewer than half (42 percent) can name at least five of the Ten Commandments; and only 11 percent read the Bible on a regular basis.

There is a crying need for Biblical knowledge! The Sunday school is uniquely structured and ready to meet this need. People are looking for a systematic study of God's Word, and not something that man has to say, either. Whether you are into an elective system or following a quarterly curriculum, involve your people in a continuing, systematic study of God's Word. Share with them the implications of the Word for today's world. God is contemporary and relevant to our times!

Publicize the fact that in your church there is, and will be, a continuing study of the Bible. People are looking for outlets of the truth. Biblical knowledge provides the foundation for living as well as the key to a better society for tomorrow, if the Lord tarries. "Line upon line, precept upon precept . . . " is the challenge to impart the living Word. It should be shared with the oldest on down to the youngest. Out of a knowledge of the Word will come the continuing thrust for evangelism as well as existence.

THE SUNDAY SCHOOL CAN APPEAL TO A WIDE VARIETY OF PEOPLE

"Touch people in as many places as possible and as many interests as possible" is a definition of evangelism. Classes can be tailored to appeal to every interest need of your community. This will entail a gathering of some knowledge about where your audience is coming from. You need to discover their "felt-need" subjects. For example, if you have a high percentage of young married couples, a class that deals with marriage adjustments and the care and feeding of young children may be the ticket that appeals.

We are told that new classes grow faster than existing classes and an average class will reach its maximum growth within 18 to 24 months. Also, every new worker on a staff will add 10 new people to your enrollment in a short time. These are axioms that have been used to build many kinds of churches. They may prove to be an added incentive to help you decide to minister to these areas of need.

Are you meeting the special needs of your people? How about a singles ministry? What do you have to offer to women? Are you ministering to the needs of the once-marrieds? Where do your oldsters fit in your ministry? Do you have a class for money management (who doesn't need it in today's world?) or homemaking or other interest needs? Do you have handicapped that need help? With an "elective" setup for adult areas, you will have a versatility that can be changed every quarter. Selection of new subject matter as well as new teachers can be very desirable changes. The possibilities are limitless as a church becomes sensitive to people's needs and ways to meet them through your Sunday school.

THE SUNDAY SCHOOL MINISTERS TO THE ENTIRE FAMILY

Encompass every age-level and minister to them at their level of maturity. There are many parents who select a church home on the basis of the ministry a particular congregation will have to their children. The teaching of the Word is the catalyst for change in the life-style of any family. What an opportunity we have to enhance and strengthen the family! Do careful research and I dare say you will find that the weekly trip to Sunday school may be the one activity in a week your families do as families. It may surprise you to find that this is the only togetherness project in many homes.

While we teach the Word and make the Word the center of our curriculum, be aware that we are teaching people. Through the Sunday school lives can be changed, homes strengthened and improved, marriages become more meaningful, personal weaknesses overcome, and families learn how to live in harmony—all because of the active ingredient—Jesus Christ.

These kinds of results will attract others who are curious as to how it all happened. And more numerical growth will result! It is impossible to be in a ministry of giving without experiencing the corresponding blessing of God on your effort. The world wants results, and the church that is producing changes in family living will reap the joys of sharing with an ever-increasing audience.

I received a phone call from a professional man who was quite well-known in our town. He began, "Pastor, what are you doing at your church?" Immediately all kinds of thoughts flooded my mind about something bad we had done or some person who had been offended. Groping for some additional time to compose myself, I said, "Please explain."

He started laughing as he replied, "Shouldn't have scared you like that! But I have an employee that has changed so much since going to your church that she will no longer lie for me! I need that kind of influence in my life. In fact, she is happy with her husband, too. And I need that kind of help for my life. . . . What time is your service next Sunday? Because I plan on coming, too." He did, and he became part of our church family and found the same kind of changes happened in his life as well.

Everywhere you turn today, the family structure is being torn down. What an opportunity for our churches to fill this ever-widening gap. If one of your purposes is to change lives, you will change family life also. The Sunday school has the ability to touch the life of every single family member—capitalize on this fact.

THE SUNDAY SCHOOL IS THE NATURAL ORGANIZATION FOR EVANGELISM

Most churches have no other organized structure with which to handle the job of evangelism and conserving the harvest. How else can you equip and train large numbers of people at the same time? You already have a trained staff that is experienced and ready to tackle this assignment of evangelizing.

Many churches are involved in "home fellowship groups" and use these for evangelism. This is an excellent answer where you have a large percentage of participation. But few churches have that strong an outreach in this area.

Sunday school is still the best organization within the church for moving into the priority of evangelism. You have the controlled situation which is best for imparting the needed challenge. It might be that your present organization and people need a new challenge or restructuring of priorities. Don't throw out the Sunday school yet. It's still the best area of ministering evangelism that we already have!

THE SUNDAY SCHOOL CAN PRESERVE THE RESULTS OF EVANGELISM

Here again we are back to the need for assimilation of new people into a permanent and growing relationship. New people that have been reached through your church must be enrolled and know for a fact that they are now part of your church body. Just as every new baby needs a home, every new "born-again" babe needs to be made part of a spiritual home. Make these new ones an entry on your records so they will be followed up if they miss a Sunday and will be included in outside-of-class functions; it will give them a sense of belonging. And make sure they receive any publications or items you use in welcoming and follow-up. Assign each new member to the care of an older member for a buddy system of caring.

Teaching they receive will become a natural part of the discipling process, interaction will reinforce their life experience, witnessing will be encouraged, and fellowship will nurture them. And the challenge to reproduce themselves can be an ongoing emphasis in each class setting.

What good will it do to win the world if we don't retain them for the Kingdom? This is one of the primary reasons God has ordained the local church to be the vehicle through which this world is to be saved. The birth process is fantastic, but the preservation of that newborn person must be as vital a part of evangelism. I wonder how many people have found Christ as Saviour only to be left on their own and eventually fall away because of failure in teaching or a lack of love or encouragement—which they could have been given by another more mature Christian?

It's been said, "Becoming a Christian is the miracle of the

moment, but the making of a saint is the process of a lifetime." The church is to be vitally involved in both processes—birth and maturation of new Christians. There is a constant struggle to keep these priorities in focus.

Parable of the Orange Tree

A number of years ago, John White wrote a "parable" about the difficulty of keeping our priorities on the right track. There must be constant evaluation to make sure our mission is on target. I've taken some editorial license to condense and update it. Here is my version of the "parable of the orange tree" for your contemplation.

I dreamed I drove on a lonely road, straight and empty. On either side were groves of orange trees; row after row stretching back from the road with boughs heavy with the round yellow fruit. It was harvesttime.

My wonderment grew as the miles slipped by. How would the harvest be gathered? During all the hours I had driven, I had seldom seen another person. The groves were empty of people, with only an occasional orange picker far from the highway. It seemed an impossible task for the very few scattered pickers. It seemed as though the earth was shaking with silent laughter at the hopelessness of the task.

Shadows were lengthening when, without warning, the road turned and there was a sign: "Leaving Neglected Country . . . Entering Home Country." The contrast was truly startling. People were everywhere and traffic was heavy. The orange groves were still there, with orange trees in abundance, and the groves were filled with multitudes of people who were happy and singing.

I parked my car and mingled with the crowd. There were smart gowns, expensive suits—everyone seemed so bright and fresh. It was a contrast to my own work clothing.

"Is it a holiday?" I asked a well-dressed woman with whom I fell in step. She looked startled, then her face relaxed in condescension, "You're a stranger, aren't you?" Before I could reply, she went on, "This is Orange Day."

She must have seen my look and continued, "It's so good to turn aside from one's labors and pick oranges one day of the week."

"But don't you pick oranges every day?" I asked.

"Yes, one must always be ready to pick oranges, but Orange Day is the day set aside to do it," she answered.

Most of the people were carrying a book beautifully bound in leather, edged in gold, and titled, *Orange Picker's Manual.*

Around one of the orange trees, seats had been arranged in tiers and they were almost full. A well-dressed man conducted me to a seat.

There were numbers of people. One man up front was talking to the people and they began to sing. The songbook was called *Songs of the Orange Groves.* The man in front admonished us to sing louder.

I was puzzled. "When do we start to pick oranges?" I asked the man who shared the songbook.

"It's not long now," he told me. "We like to get everyone warmed up first. . . . Besides, we want to make the oranges feel at home."

I thought he was joking. After a while, a rather fat man read two sentences from his well-worn copy of the *Orange Picker's Manual* and began to make a speech. I wasn't sure if he was talking to the people or oranges.

I looked around and saw a number of similar groups gathered around other trees here and there, being addressed by other fat men. Some trees had no one around them.

"Which trees do we pick from?" I asked the man beside me. He didn't seem to understand, so I pointed to the trees around about.

"This is our tree," he said.

"But there are too many of us to pick from just one tree," I protested. "There are more people than oranges!"

"We don't pick oranges," the man patiently explained, "we haven't been called. That's the Pastor Orange Picker's job. We're here to support him. Besides we haven't been to Manual School. You need to know how an orange thinks before you can pick it successfully."

"What's Manual School?" I whispered.

"It's where they go to study the *Orange Picker's Manual,*" my informant went on, "it takes years to understand it."

The fat man in the front was still making his speech. His face was red and he seemed indignant about some of the rival groups. But then a glow came on his face, "We are not forsaken," he said. "We have much to be thankful for. Last week we saw three oranges brought into the baskets and we are now debt-free, having paid off the new cushions you sit on."

The man in front was reaching a climax; the atmosphere seemed tense. Then with a dramatic gesture he reached for two of the oranges, plucked them from the branch, and placed them in a basket at his feet. The applause was deafening.

"Do we start picking now?" I asked my informant.

"What do you think we're doing?" he hissed. "What do you think this tremendous effort has been made for? There's more orange-picking talent in this group than in the rest of Home Country."

I apologized quickly, "I don't want to be critical. The man in front must be an excellent orange picker. But surely the rest of us could try! There are so many oranges that need picking. We've got hands; we can read the manual!"

"When you've been in the business as long as I have, you'll realize it's not that simple," he replied. "There isn't time. We have work to do and families to care for. We. . . ."

But I wasn't listening. It began to dawn on me. Whatever these people were, they were not orange pickers. Orange picking was a form of weekend entertainment. I tried one or two more of the groups. Not all had such high academic standards; some held classes on orange picking. I tried to tell them of the trees I had seen in Neglected Country, but no one had any interest.

The sun was setting in my dream as I drove back along the road I had come. All around me were the vast, empty orange groves. But there had been changes. . . . Everywhere the ground was littered with fallen fruit; it seemed as though the trees had rained oranges to the ground, where they lay rotting.

I thought of all the people in Home Country. Then, booming through the trees, there came a voice which said, "The harvest truly is plenteous, but the laborers are few; pray ye therefore the Lord of the harvest, that he will send forth laborers. . . ."

And I awakened, for it was only a dream!

9

Evangelism in the Classroom

The last command of our Lord was: "Go . . . and teach"! The teaching task involves a twofold challenge: to teach so that people might be brought into fellowship with God (the evangelism function), and to teach those brought into the fellowship in the ways they should be walking.

From the very moment a person becomes a follower of Christ, he not only is a learner but also must be a responsible spokesman for the gospel of Christ. All are to be involved whenever and wherever there is an opportunity. In a general but vital sense, every Christian is called to be a teacher.

Our focus will be on the Sunday school as one place where a servant of the Lord can obey the clear call to "teach." In the context of our study, we are most concerned about the first of this twofold function: teaching so that people are evangelized; teaching so they find Jesus Christ as Lord; teaching so there will be a life-changing experience. Teaching has always had a prominent role in God's redemptive plan. We are facing a time when the need for competent communicators has never been more critical.

This chapter will deal with some of the principles and methods that can be used to make teaching the kind that will be reaching for decisions. We'll be looking at factors that must come together so the classroom can be an effective place for evangelism.

The Priority

What do you want to have happen in your class this coming Sunday? In what direction will your teaching be pointed? Will you be only teaching the lesson or are you going to be reaching for souls? At the close of that precious hour, do you plan to leave with a sense of accomplishment or leave in defeat because you were sidetracked?

There are many things you can accomplish in the class. Keep in mind that nearly anyone can read the teacher's quarterly to a class of students, but real teaching for decision is much more than such an exercise in futility. Again, what do you plan to have happen in your class? You may think you want great things to happen, but you only have a limited time span. To make the best use of those few minutes will take an effort in planning—to make them count for eternity.

SET A GOAL FOR THIS WEEK

You could teach with the goal of increasing Biblical knowledge. This is an excellent and worthy goal. Knowledge is knowing, recognizing, and communicating facts. It's one of the requirements for the successful Christian life. It should be an ongoing goal. It takes more than one class session to teach the major spiritual truths, much less the entire gamut of God's Word.

Or, you can teach with the goal of changing an attitude. It's a worthy goal for any lesson. Attitudes are based on emotions, feelings, understanding, and value judgments. These are built on the foundation of knowledge.

Have you taught with the goal of effecting a behavioral change? Behavior is what one does, how one solves the problem, how one treats people, and how one acts in the light of basic knowledge.

Knowing what God says about all believers being brothers and sisters in the family is a fact that can be learned because it can be taught. The ultimate learning of this truth happens when your pupils not only think in these terms, but also begin to act to serve others in this kind of relationship. Knowledge is only that until it is translated into a life-changing action.

When you teach for a goal, everything you do is geared in that direction. Too much of our classroom teaching can best be described as being like the man who flung himself on his horse and rode off in all directions at the same time!

In the light of our subject at hand, evangelism in the classroom would be the highest goal you could set! At this point you will be effecting life changes for time as well as eternity. You will be turning people from the ways of sin to a new direction to follow God. That's the definition of true repentance, " a complete turning around of direction and returning in the opposite way." As the little girl said, "It's being sorry enough for your sins to quit doing them."

Evangelism is a goal that comes directly out of the heartthrob of God: "The Lord is . . . not willing that any should perish, but that all should come to repentance" (2 Peter 3:9). This was the singular goal of Jesus Christ: "For this cause came I unto this hour" (John 12:27). The cause was Calvary, which in turn became the vehicle of salvation for the entire world.

Evangelism is not the by-product of classroom efforts. It should be the goal, the very purpose for being. It is the reason for the entire Church to exist. Therefore, the first and most important decision you, as a teacher, will make is the classroom objective, your teaching/learning goal. My challenge to you is to make evangelism the primary goal this week and in the weeks to come.

The Teacher

God has always used people in carrying out His purpose in reaching the lost and will continue to do so. There are no "plan B's" on the drawing board; no alternative plans to use angels or any kind of being other than mankind.

The most vital factor we will look at in this chapter is the wonderful creature called the teacher! The call of today is not for better methods, but better people! So our quest is to delve into the innermost being of that beautiful person who is a teacher. Surveys confirm the classroom teacher as the most important element in each situation. He/she is the most critical element to make all the chemistry jell for the right results.

Meaningful teaching is more than using the latest methods, the finest materials, the most sophisticated approaches, or the most dramatics. To be a teacher is to be growing in understanding and insight, because the teacher is first and foremost a learner, too.

TEACHING IS A TRUST

Teaching takes on meaning with the realization that it is a trust from God. It is more than teacher's work. Paul informs the church at Thessalonica: "We were allowed of God to be put in trust with the gospel, even so we speak; not as pleasing men, but God" (1 Thessalonians 2:4). It's important that each teacher work from this divine motivation.

Your response to God will be evident in your teaching. The teaching experience will invariably reveal to your class the most meaningful relationship in your life. If the teacher has responded to God in faithfulness, love, and consistency, then this is what will be revealed before the class; in fact, you can't hide this. Out of that life-changing experience with God will come a teaching style that has the same kind of impact on others.

DIRECT THEM TO GOD

One of the tasks of a teacher is to direct a learner's response to God, rather than to the teacher or another person. A teacher who has experienced the joys of daily living for Christ, who has felt and is walking in a vital growing discipleship with God, will produce the same in those who are exposed in the class. You've heard it said, "A stream cannot rise higher than its source."

A teacher's purpose is to open up channels and doorways for his/her students to help their walk with God. This style of teaching will reveal Jesus Christ as the supreme revelation of God's redeeming love. In turn, they will want to share this revelation with others. A vital teacher will have vital followers; a witnessing instructor will have witnessing students.

I was standing at the door of our church, greeting the congregation as they left the sanctuary after the morning service, when a relatively new family came by. I greeted each member and shook hands with them. The mother asked her little girl, about age 4, if she would please tell the pastor what had happened in her class that morning. Without a moment's hesitation she blurted out, "I saw Jesus in our class today!"

The mother volunteered, "She didn't really see Jesus, but thought her teacher was Jesus." What a beautiful thing to have happen in each class! Later I went to the teacher, a man who had led the class in worship as part of their extended session, and related to him the conversation at the church door.

He looked at me, and I saw tears of joy appear in his eyes as he replied, "Pastor, that was my prayer this morning before I entered that classroom. . . . 'Don't let them see me, but let them see Jesus'!"

REACH FOR SOULS EVERY WEEK

Can you think of a better setting for evangelism than in your classroom? Evangelistic teaching comes out of that vital, exciting experience each teacher must have with Jesus Christ. Teaching is the process of reproducing the life of Christ in others.

The teacher, to be effective, will be prepared and relevant. The gospel is a message without change, but the methods must be contemporary in order to have a hearing. All of life's experiences can contribute to the contemporary class. Making disciples in today's world means helping the student find solutions to life. And the ultimate solution to a confusing, senseless life is Jesus! Teacher, what a fantastic privilege you have! What an exciting opportunity you have each Sunday. Read the challenge as expressed in this short poem:

> *When I enter that beautiful city . . .*
> *And the saints in glory draw near,*
> *I want someone to greet me and tell me,*
> *It was you who invited me here!*

Author Unknown

What an exciting thought! The privilege of inviting people to make heaven their eternal home is waiting for you in your class this coming week!

The Student

"How shall I begin?" is one of the first questions confronting most teachers. The manner in which you look upon the persons in your class will have a great bearing as to how this question will be answered by you. Do you see your class as a bunch of dummies who know nothing, and consider yourself the superior all-knowing being who will be dispensing all they learn? If you view your pupils in this manner, you might as well stay at home next week and save your energy! On the other hand, if you see them as having worth because they are part of God's very special creation, and consider yourself a part of this group who will be learning and growing together in the grace and knowledge of our Lord, you will experience success.

Each person must be cherished by the teacher just as he or she is, because of our Creator. This may mean you will have the privilege of knowing and loving your pupils in a deeper way than any other person in the church. The learner is not just a number to be posted on the attendance roll, he/she is not just a machine; each one is a whole, wonderful, different, total person who needs understanding. It goes without saying that love is the greatest of gifts a teacher can give.

This book is too short to look at all the specific characteristics you will find at each age-level. There are some general things that will warrant a look simply as a reminder. Keep these in mind for utilizing the learning process at different age-levels. If communication is the process of one person speaking to another in a language common to both, it follows that you will use a different approach at the varied ages.

CHARACTERISTICS OF CHILDREN

Dividing children into properly graded groups recognizes their level of understanding and the influence that peers will exert on them. Effective teachers will make use of seeing, touching, smelling, tasting, and hearing in this classroom.

Abstract truths can be more easily understood through the use of objects or pictures. Sensory experiences will sharpen and speed the learning process for children. Children think in terms of themselves, their family, and other things that are close to them. So, the teacher will have to be careful to use "life-related" terminology.

Children are changing rapidly; they are more urbanized and

mobile. Families live in one place for shorter periods of time. Many families are fragmenting, so some of your kids may have multiple parents or foster parents. Kids who have spent their lives in the city don't even know what a farm is all about, so they can't grasp some of the concepts from the Word (especially when it talks about sheep or sowing seed, for example). It's not news to you, either, to know the average high school graduate will have spent 12,000 hours in a public classroom and, during that same time span, 15,000 hours in front of a television set! (That's about 2 full years of nonstop TV viewing.) We are competing with the media age.

The years of childhood are the foundational years, and all the child learns here, he will build on for the rest of his life. Through your expression of love, understanding, and the use of the right materials and correct techniques, children can be led to a warm, meaningful relationship with Jesus Christ! Don't underestimate the importance of your ministry to children. To see a child saved is to save an entire life. "Train up a child in the way he should go . . ." and walk that way yourself in leading them to Christ.

CHARACTERISTICS OF YOUTH

Dealing with youth is a different "bag" (to use one of their terms). Immediate relevancy and interaction are but two of the key factors in understanding youth. A survey was taken among some youth who had left their churches and the most common reaction was, "I didn't think the church was very important."

Teens are exciting people to minister to. You will find they want to be treated like adults. Youth are in the process of maturation physically in these years. They face problems in social adjustments. They want some kind of restraints, but at the same time they resent these restraints. Teens are unpredictable. At this juncture of life, before they are really prepared, they are faced with some real serious life choices. They are wondering what they will do with their lives, whom they might marry, who they are becoming, and whether or not to go on to college. They are searching and floundering about, trying to establish some life goals. At the same time, they are trying their

wings on the way to independence. They are in need of building a solid theory of life.

Youth need to know about the stabilizing influence of Jesus
Christ when He is made the Lord of one's life. The most
important relationship you can lead your youth in establishing
is one with Jesus Christ. They all seem to be in need of encouragement and lots of love. Young people are looking for understanding friends. One of the most important things you can give
to a teenager is acceptance; he or she craves this. They are
caught in a constant struggle with the feeling of being "left out"
of life.

"Remember now thy Creator in the days of thy youth . . . "
(Ecclesiastes 12:1) was the admonition from the wisest man
this world has ever seen; his name was Solomon. Your ministry
to teens is the key to letting that happen. Teens need Jesus
Christ to be a living reality, and you as a teacher can be the
person who makes it work.

CHARACTERISTICS OF ADULTS

Grown-ups are concerned about the business of living life in
a real world. Many of the illusions of youth have been placed
aside or knocked down by the nitty-gritty give-and-take of their
world. It's not an easy place in which to live and feel productive.

We are faced with ever-growing personal problems in today's
adult. Some of these difficulties have arisen as an aftermath of
broken homes; broken homes have left broken people.

Another segment that is growing in size is the senior citizen
population. Loneliness, fear, worry about tomorrow, and rejection are all things with which these adults are trying to cope.
The population of our nation, as a whole, is getting older each
passing year, and these adults need Jesus Christ. There is an
urgency because of the shortness of their remaining life.

EACH INDIVIDUAL IS IMPORTANT

The student is a huge factor in making every classroom a
place of evangelism. How could you make your appeal if there
were no one present to hear it? Each person is unique in the
plan and purpose of God. Look at the individual as God must

look at him, for each person is a rarity; there is only one of each person. Consider a painting by Rembrandt, a bronze by Degas, a violin by Stradivarius, or a play by Shakespeare. These have great value for two reasons: their creators were masters, and these masterpieces are few in number. Yet, each of these masters created more than one of the items for which he is so famous.

Each person is the most valuable treasure on the face of the earth, because we know who created each human being and there is only one of each! Never in all the billions of humans who have walked on the earth from the beginning of time has there been another person like you or me or any of the people to whom you will minister!

People are rebelling against the impersonal system of this world. People are more than a number to be filed, folded, or stapled. Christ was talking about His relationship to His own sheep in the story that is recorded by John. We're interested in a single line: "He calleth his own sheep by name" (John 10:3). The gospel restores dignity and meaning to life. Let there be an awareness of the importance of the individual in each class. Each is one of a kind, the rarest of the rare, a priceless treasure possessed of qualities of mind and speech, and appearance and actions, unlike any other person who has lived, now lives, or shall live!

"For . . . what shall a man give in exchange for his soul?" (Mark 8:36, 37). By implication, Jesus is saying a person's soul is worth more than this entire world; there is nothing that could buy it. You will be facing some of these priceless treasures next Sunday as you enter the classroom to do battle for their souls! May God grant that we never lose sight of the importance of the student in our process of evangelism.

The Curriculum

Curriculum is defined by Webster as "a prescribed course of study in a school." Let's expand on it and read it this way: "that which is happening under guidance toward the objective in a church."

Planning of curriculum must be part of a unified plan based on the objectives of an individual church. It's not necessary for the individual teacher to be an expert in the many phases of curriculum planning, but it is necessary for him/her to see the unity and completeness of the total plan in which he/she is to function.

Provide Curriculum to Meet Specific Needs

For example, suppose you are teaching the seventh-grade class and your concern is with the special needs of this group. You will want to know what resources are available to be specific enough to reach those needs. Everything you do must reflect the life needs of these early teens.

Also, be aware of the fact that you are a teacher in a community of believers who have been drawn together because of their common faith and doctrine. You want to fulfill your responsibility in line with your doctrinal distinctives, so you consider the fact that your class is part of the larger whole.

Then, too, your charges are part of a family which, in turn, is part of the church. Your students do more in the life of your church than attend a church school class once each week. Every person in your class has something in common with all the other participants in that congregation. In your church, then, the curriculum plan must be a reflection of the common objective. In our case, this common objective is the salvation of lost souls through the classroom ministry.

Use a Unified Curriculum

Fortunately for us, our own Gospel Publishing House has provided a unified curriculum for the entire gamut of material needed for every age-group. Their *Word of Life* lesson materials will carry through an overriding theme that is exciting and totally integrated with each level of learning. Beyond that, these materials reflect our philosophies and distinctives, such as the Holy Spirit, the Spirit-filled life, and more. We do not have to make a special effort to include doctrinal distinctives, for they are written and planned with you and your church needs in mind.

If you are into "adult electives," there is an excellent variety of teaching materials already prepared in the *Radiant Life Series.* Each has a student's book as well as a teacher's guide.

You will find these materials are being constantly upgraded and are contemporary.

We have some of the very best in curriculum materials available to any group of churches anywhere. You can solve your curriculum selection problems by staying with our own publishing house. This way, you are assured that children, youth, and adults will have a well-rounded, in-depth study based on God's Word. Try it, you'll like it!

SUPPORTIVE MATERIALS

In addition to the curriculum you have selected, each teacher should build an ever-growing collection of materials to enhance teaching. Learning is not automatic but relates directly to the pupil's motivation. The teacher can secure such motivation through the use of interest-building and idea-conveying materials. These can relate to lesson content as well as the method or application of lesson truth. I'm referring to such things as books, observation of people, illustrations, written notes, personal experiences, and object lessons.

Try an "illustration file." Fill it with "windows" that are clear, interesting, appropriate, and easily understood. An illustration lets the light dawn. Place these clippings in a file and arrange them in topical order, then use them.

Do you have an "idea garden"? It might take the form of a spiral notebook in which you have placed ideas you have heard. Some ideas may be original with you; others may be borrowed from another successful source. These are "planted" to bring forth a later harvest.

The "picture file" is very important for the little people, especially the 4-, 5-, and 6-year-olds. It's still true that a picture is worth about a thousand words. It is simple, but it still works. Cut pictures from magazines, newspapers, or handout papers.

Do you have your own reference library? Every teacher should have a minimum of two supplementary reference books—a concordance and a Bible dictionary. Any additional resources relating to Bible history, geography, or biographies can add to your effectiveness as a teacher.

LESSON PLANNING

No teacher is really prepared to stand before a class without some kind of a plan. This can take a variety of forms, but there are some items basic to almost all lesson planning. The bare bones should include the approach (or introduction), the body, and a conclusion. Also make note of the materials to be used, the method you have selected, and the application. By all means, make an evaluation after each lesson with an eye to making improvements for the next session.

Remember this: the effective teacher plans for almost all the learning experiences taking place in the class. The teacher lays plans for evangelism! We could turn that around to say that no evangelism takes place without planning and preparation.

Curriculum is a vital part of your total game plan and fills an important place in the total evangelism experience.

Expect Results

Expect people to be saved! Believe that it will happen through your ministry. Pray with an urgency about the souls you claim for the Kingdom. How many people have been saved in your class this past year? two years? five years? ten years?

You will sow what you reap. You may have been thinking of reaping in terms of an eternal reward, but you don't have to wait for eternity. You are in a position to reap a harvest every Sunday morning, as well as every day, through your extended ministry through the efforts of your class. What have you sown in the past? If you teach next week and expect everything to be the same as usual, that is what you will have. Some people have very low expectations because they do not want to be disappointed. Effective teaching can be measured by the results. These results will be classroom evangelism, daily witnessing, numerical growth, spiritual growth in individual lives, changed lives and more!

I wish I had the eloquence to challenge you in such a way that you would never get away from the priority called evangelism! Evangelism has its place in your classroom every single week! But it is not to be confined to Sundays only. We are engaged in a battle for the eternal souls of men, women, boys, and girls!

There Is an Urgency

Come with me to the very turn of our century, 1903 to be exact, and the fire at the Iroquois Theatre. Eddie Foy was there in a huge extravaganza; the place was packed with people. Fire broke out and seemed to explode as it filled and enveloped the building.

Panic struck immediately! People jammed the aisles in a desperate struggle to get to the doors. Hot gases and smoke filled the place, turning it into a death chamber, and 590 people died. It was an awful scene. The strong showed no mercy as they shoved aside the weak. People literally climbed over the bodies of others as they clawed their way to freedom. Some made their escape over the mountain of bodies blocking the exits.

We're interested in the story of one man who made his way out of the inferno. He didn't live long afterwards; the horror and shock affected him deeply. As he reached the end of his days, he would go into his room and shut the door. His worried family would come and listen, only to hear him cry out again and again in his agony, "I saved no one but myself! I saved no one but myself!" He kept this up until he died. What a way to go out of this life into eternity!

There is an analogy here. One of these days this world and world system will go up in flames (2 Peter 3:9-13). The only place of safety is in Jesus Christ. As a Sunday school worker, you have given your life to Christ, you have found the place of safety, but how many could you take with you? Life must be lived with an eye on eternity; classroom evangelism is not something to play at. It's a serious business because we are dealing with the souls of people and a soul is extremely precious—it will never die! We're in a world that is heading for hell. Multitudes who do not know Jesus Christ as Saviour will not escape the destruction ahead, unless you tell them!

There is a great adventure ahead for you as you turn your class into an evangelistic outreach. God has promised you His power, which will be unleashed through your life and ministry:

But ye shall receive power, after that the Holy Ghost is come upon you: and ye shall be witnesses unto me both in [the *classroom*] Jerusalem, . . . and unto the uttermost part of the earth (Acts 1:8).

10

The Challenge for the Future in Christian Education

The future—ready or not it's coming! It always arrives whether or not you are ready or expecting it. You have no way of predicting what will happen a year from now, let alone tomorrow, yet yesterday's future is our today!

What is ahead for this world? By the same implication, what is the church facing? "Futurists" are a whole new group of social scientists and experts who look into the future to seek to explore it with the thought of anticipating what might be, as well as developing alternatives to handle the future.

Robert Jungk, professor of planning sciences at the Technical University located in Berlin, said: "Power belongs to those who can anticipate the future." Andre van Dam, corporate planner for CPC International, Inc., in Buenos Aires, says: "Everything affects everything else."

A split image of the future world seems to be emerging among those who look into the future. On the one hand, they are projecting astonishing advances in medicine that could vanquish cancer and delay the aging process, developments in agriculture that could provide food for the world from the Arctic and by farming the oceans, and transportation systems that could whisk huge loads of passengers around the world and even into space.

Futurists also see a negative side: climatic conditions will be changing, resulting in a hotter, drier, dirtier, and even more crowded world. They see an increase of crime, famine, terrorism, and family breakups, with all kinds of alternative lifestyles. Whatever actually happens, they are agreed, this world will experience drastic changes socially, economically, and population wise. There will be vast changes, and the future world will, without doubt, be a much different world.

The day is coming (predicted to happen by 1990) when 80 percent of American homes will have computers that assist in doing homework for the kids, balancing the family budget, taking care of the climate controls of the home, doing the shopping, offering entertainment options at the touch of a switch, and providing banking services. And doctors will be able to make electronic house calls! It will soon be possible to connect every home on the face of the earth by computer links and communication satellites.

Many people see tomorrow as an extension of today, forgetting the future is touched by trends and these trends don't continue in straight lines. Points are reached at which they explode into new phenomena. Direction can be reversed; new ones may start or stop—nothing remains unchanged. The future is much like a liquid.

The Future Population

Look at the population projected. In 1900, only a handful of cities had a population of 1 million or more. By the year 2000, there will be several hundred cities with a million or more and these will have such strange-sounding names as Ogbomosho in Nigeria and Kananga in Zaire! United Nations population projections are that the new century will have 67 cities of 1 million or more in China alone, and the world's largest city will be Mexico City, with 31 million! The projected world population will be 6 billion, with more than half living in cities for the first time in world history.

In 1900 when the world contained 1.6 billion people, only 1 out of 100 people lived in an urban setting. This growing migration of people to the cities is caused by their desire to have available the sources of education, better health care, and more job opportunities. This trend is greatest in Africa, India, and parts of Asia.

The Family Unit Is Undergoing Stress

Family structure is changing. I point to only one movement, the explosion of "solos" or singles. In the United States in 1970, there were 1.5 million persons living alone, but by 1978 there were 4.3 million. Today, about one-fifth of all households are composed of people living alone. An increasing number of people are opting for living together and not bothering about the formalities of making the marriage legal.

Society is moving from a child-centered to an adult-centered home as a result of the rising age-level of older Americans. There are the "aggregate" family units in which divorced people with children remarry to form a new home. Only 7 percent of our population now live in the traditional family setting (working husband, wife who is a homemaker, and two children). Marriage in the future will encompass a number of options by people who want different things from their relationships with each other.

People, on the one hand, are saying that advancing technology will help us cope with the exploding needs of this planet, while others predict we will be worse off in the coming century. Alvin Toffler, author of *Future Shock* (New York: Bantam Books, Inc., 1971) gives this word of warning: "Under conditions of high-speed change, a democracy without the ability to anticipate condemns itself to death." The future is a challenge.

The Church Must Anticipate, Too

What does all this mean to the Church? What's in store for the Church in America and around the world? The opportunity for unprecedented growth! It will happen only if God's people redeem the time, pray to the Lord of the harvest for direction, and dedicate themselves, as well as all their resources, to the appropriate action in harvesting this great "field white unto harvest."

Christian education in Assemblies of God churches has long been on the cutting edge of evangelism and the vehicle of change for meeting the challenges of the present day. Exciting changes have taken place as the church, through its arm of education, has met the needs that have arisen. There are changes with all kinds of implications to meet again, if the Church is to be contemporary to this day and age. Please look at some of the challenges of the future.

The Challenge to Use the Communications Media

Jesus Christ was the most effective communicator who ever lived! He was contemporary to His day, as He made use of available techniques and invented a few of His own. Christ wrote on the sand, questioned some of His listeners, allowed himself to be questioned, healed people, made clay to anoint a blind man's eyes, painted vivid word pictures, and had an appeal to His audiences, which were made up of all classes of people. The Holy Spirit is infinite variety as He moves through and energizes yielded people. He can be the source for incredible ideas as to how to use the media to evangelize people through the vast new vistas of change in this one area.

In the classroom, one challenge is: How can you get them to listen after they've been watching TV? Why not plan on using the same approach? With the video cassette recorder coming on the scene, the possibilities for classroom use are endless. Check it out. You'll find it isn't too costly an enterprise, and I predict that they will reduce in price as they become more common. Think of the excitement that could be generated if you were studying the story of the Good Samaritan, for example. You could have your class roleplay the story, while using other people from your class to run the camera and record this impromptu production. Can you imagine the interest as you play back their efforts on the monitor? A total learning experience involving the eye gate, ear gate, and actual participation will greatly increase the retention of the pupil.

Consider this application in an adult class. The VCR is set up for your lecture on "How to Receive the Baptism in the Holy Spirit." Your lecture is recorded and placed in your video library for future use. For each class member missing because of sickness, another person could reproduce the tape for playback on the monitor at home or in the hospital room, to share the day's lesson. Or, consider the visitor to your church who may be interested in the baptism in the Holy Spirit. Simply take that visitor to check out the tape on the Holy Spirit lecture, and use the monitor available in a booth for that purpose. There he will see and hear the full lecture and receive the same impact as in the class. The possibilities are unlimited.

Or, what would be wrong with your church having its own

mini-UHF station or a cable linkup with every church member's home? There is the possibility of having a microwave system. People who want to receive your telecast would become part of the system by renting a receiver placed on their home TV set.

There is a crying need for better materials to use in Christian programming, especially for children's viewing. Perhaps your school could be the pioneer in developing new methods of distribution. You could supply a series of tapes about your church, doctrines, or services to an area distributor for the home-computer retrievable system. Then people would be able to dial a number to receive your telecast on any subject of interest.

We've just scratched the surface of the future in communications affecting us. In the past we have often rejected new developments and refused to use them. We live in the age of the electronic media. We must not confuse the message with the medium, because we have the most powerful message that can be distributed to others. The message of the gospel can be communicated with contemporary methods.

Let's put aside one fear you may have. The "electronic church" will never replace the need for a strong, vital, loving, and vibrant local church. TV, great as it is, will never replace people-to-people interaction.

The Challenge of Ministering to Family and Personal Needs

The family is in trouble today. We could cite numerous surveys to confirm what we already know. The basic structure and fabric around which the family was formed is under attack by this world system and the mover behind this system, Satan. If the family can be destroyed, society has no other institution on which it can be built. The Church has help for the troubled family! Attack on the family unit goes all the way back to the first couple in the Garden of Eden, and has continued on down to this day with an accelerated barrage.

Each segment of the home needs the strength and support the church can give it. Children are the products of broken homes in too many families. There is an increase of fragmented families, with problems such as a need for self-identity, rejection, guilt, lack of purpose—the church needs to address these.

If we have nothing else in our educational program, at least let there be an outpouring of divine love in such a way that every person will know that God loves families as well as the individuals in the family.

Your class may be the only place where some children will ever experience love. The Sunday school hour might be the only segment of a child's life when he/she can see an adult who is a worthy model after which a life can be patterned. Children are coming to our schools with deep needs reflecting the tragedies of today. Children, ages 5, 6, and 7 are having ulcers! Kids with serious psychological problems, unable to cope with outrageous conditions, will look to the church for any kind of help or relief. To meet the "people" needs facing us, we must make our teaching the most effective we ever have.

Have you addressed yourself to the singles in your town? Here is a growing segment of the population that has some desperate needs. We again call it to your attention that approximately 20 percent of all the people in your community are single. Many of these are shattered people who have been divorced or have survived the death of a spouse. Facing them are loneliness, frustration, guilt, fear, rejection, and the need for economic security. And many of them are still working their way through the trauma of a broken home. The church can effectively reach out to these; perhaps by having a class for singles, a full-time minister to singles, or a social activities program. There is also a corresponding number of single-parent homes—family units with only one parent who has to try to do the job of two. Ministry to singles can take many forms, but it's a ministry that we need to get on with.

There is a growing awareness among men that the function of "fathering" is changing. Christian education can minister to this need, also. God has given a pattern for the "priest" in his home and this principle is being attacked.

Teens are looking for help to withstand the pressures placed on them by peers experimenting with the drug scene, free sexual expression, and bold rebellion against the familiar order of home, family, and church.

God will work through the church to express His love for families. The family is still the all-important, God-ordained institution upon which the church will be built and society will be influenced. "As the family goes, so goes the world," aptly says it—plus, so goes the church!

To underscore the family situation, consider that the couple who marries today has about a 50-50 chance of staying married. If they divorce and remarry, the chances of making it drop to 70-30. But when the children of parents that divorce get married, they have about an 80-20 chance of making their marriage last! The family is important, and this awareness must have top priority in our Christian education. We must do all we can to enhance the family structure, as well as helping the individuals who are part of the family.

The Challenge of Meeting Contemporary Issues

Keep in mind: "Everything that happens affects everything else," and look with open minds at some of the issues on the horizon today that will become reality tomorrow. We can no longer stick our hearts in cold storage or our heads in the sand with the hope that these issues will go away.

Here are only a few of the issues affecting and confronting the future church, should the Lord tarry that long. I am posing them in the form of questions: Will there be a military draft, and should Christians have the right to resist it? What about divorce and remarriage for the believer? How should we treat this problem in our educational system? How will we handle the question of homosexuals who may want to be part of our Sunday school? Should the church take a stand on the distribution of pornography? What about the issue of abortion and government intervention?

How should the individual rights movements be handled— such as women's lib, children's rights, gay rights, black rights, animal rights, and more? Is there a right and wrong side to the reproductive engineering now possible in today's world? Should we be involved in solving world hunger? Will we open our churches so they can be of help to the misplaced and refugee peoples from the Third World? Is ecology an issue that we should be part of? Should we attack the many new doctrines coming out of the religious world? Can the cults be countered? Do we have an answer for the drug victim?

These are but a few of the contemporary problems and issues facing the church. These things will be affecting Christian educational programs. Wave after wave of movements and motions will continue to flood into our lives and ministries. Will the church capitulate from the "marketplaces" of the world or will we be in the vanguard to provide answers to the things that affect the life-style of pupils in our church? Most of these issues will not give way to simplistic answers.

The church itself is going through many changes, brought on by economic conditions as well as ecological and energy problems. Are we faced with a day when it will be impossible for people to drive to church? Are we going to be forced into the neighborhood "house" church concept? Should we be in the process of training the church to be ready to "go underground," in case conditions of this world warrant it?

In the face of inflating costs, should we be building bigger buildings or seeking to make more efficient use of the ones we already have? Could we be seeing weekday schools instead of Sunday schools? Do we see ourselves in the form of a "mother" church with numerous small, satellite neighborhood meeting places? Should we be thinking in terms of integrating all our ministries so the congregation can make a single trip to the church once each week, then supplement this with video teaching to be used in homes or neighborhood units? The list of problems is endless.

Alvin Toffler's statement should be rephrased by the church to read like this: "Under conditions of high-speed change, a church or Christian education program that is without the ability to anticipate condemns itself to death."

This information has been shared to help you to stretch as you anticipate the future. In the past, many people have tried to remain unchanged or live as they have always lived—it doesn't work. There is another factor to keep in mind: the future for the church may not be very lengthy! In the meantime, we have the admonition of Jesus who bluntly told us to "occupy till I come"! *The Jerusalem Bible* states it like this: "Do business . . . until I get back" (Luke 19:13). He also said, "I must be about my Father's business." Can we do less till He comes for His church?

There is no way all of the contemporary issues can be outlined in these few short paragraphs. And you can be sure they will become more numerous and will increase in complexity. In all of this there are Biblical solutions to life found only in Jesus Christ! There must be an awareness that God will not be caught by surprise at any new development. He is a God of infinite variety, and with heaven's direction the Church need not be sidetracked into oblivion. God is as contemporary as the future will be!

The Challenge of Evangelizing Today's World

Wouldn't you love to visit a typical church of the first century? Somehow, I believe the congregation at Ephesus or Colossae, for instance, could tell us how to have a church reach and evangelize its world.

The original command still stands! Jesus said:

> But ye shall receive power, after that the Holy Ghost is come upon you: and ye shall be witnesses unto me, both in Jerusalem, and in all Judea, and in Samaria, and unto the uttermost part of the earth (Acts 1:8).

If Jesus appeared in the flesh, in person, to give this command directly to you as He did the founders of the first church, what would your reaction be? Would you tell Him how impossible the task is? Ask yourself a question or two: What is our "Jerusalem"? What was their "Jerusalem"? What were "Judea" and "Samaria" for them and for us?

Jerusalem is the hometown—that's not too tough. Judea takes us a bit further into what we could classify as the county, state, or even nation.

What about "Samaria"? Be careful in your answer to this. Think a minute . . . Samaria was in Judea. Samaria was a racially segregated area and its people were the outcasts of their day. For us today, our "Samaria" would include the "boat people," the Indian, the immigrant, the Hispanic, the migrant, the ghetto dweller, the poor, the unlovely, the undesirable. Jesus didn't forget to include these folk for all time and our day.

The pattern for outreach is founded on the example of the first church. They didn't build buildings or hold Sunday school contests; they mobilized each person to become an evangelist for the gospel message. No inviting people to come to their church; they went into the "highways and byways to compel them to come" to Christ.

Take another look at some of our concepts. If we followed the New Testament pattern, our church buildings would not be the center of evangelism; they did not exist for the first-century church. This is not a tirade against your building or an invitation for you to burn it. This is simply an appeal to place the priority of evangelism in the right perspective.

If we are to reach the world for Jesus Christ, we must break out of the barriers called church buildings and go where the lost can be found. Church buildings may be one of the greatest hindrances to world evangelization; not because we have nice buildings, but because we don't want to get outside of them to reach a hurting world. Yes, the church building is still needed in our day, but let's not let it hinder our reaching out on behalf of others who are without Christ and hope. Your church building keeps you dry when it rains, cool when it's hot, and warm when it's cold. Your church is to be a battle station, a training center from which you send each Christian out!

It was calculated that approximately 25 percent of the world's population was identified with evangelical Christianity about 200 years ago. Today the percentage is estimated to be around 8 percent and decreasing. At the present rate of decrease, only about 2 percent of the world's population will be identified with evangelical Christianity by the year 2000—unless we reverse this trend by God's help! I believe we are seeing and experiencing a turnabout, particularly when looking at the Pentecostal message.

This trend can be illustrated in its crisis proportions by picturing two cars ready to leave New York City on the freeway system. They are on their way to California. One car moves at the rate of 10 miles per hour and the other at 100 miles per hour. We can see how quickly the car traveling at the faster rate of speed will leave the other car in its trip across this nation. The 100-m.p.h. car represents the exploding world population, while the 10-m.p.h. car represents the expansion of Christianity.

Could it be that some well-meaning persons have hijacked many churches and diverted them from their primary purpose—to reach and win the lost for Jesus Christ? Somehow we need to change direction and stop any drifting and meandering through our world and get the church back on the main road. It's not the easiest thing to do, but it must be done.

The writer Mark tells us Jesus says we are to take the gospel message to *every creature!* It's a significant detail in Mark 16:15: "You are to go into all the world and preach the Good News to *everyone, everywhere" (The Living Bible)!* It can be done in our generation! The methods employed by the New Testament Church show how it can be accomplished.

Paul writes about his *modus operandi:*

> I kept back nothing that was profitable unto you, but have showed you, and have taught you publicly, and from house to house, testifying both to the Jews, and also to the Greeks, repentance toward God, and faith toward our Lord Jesus Christ (Acts 20:20).

His game plan was "publicly, *and* from house to house. . . ." First, in mass meetings, as the Church was motivated and trained for the task, then in a house-to-house campaign.

Was it effective? Check this verse again: "And this continued by the space of two years; so that *all* they which dwelt in Asia heard the word of the Lord Jesus, both Jews and Greeks" (Acts 19:10). Think of it! In only 2 years, 24 months, 730 days, 17,520 hours, they had evangelized such teeming cities as Jerusalem (estimated to have had a population of 200,000), Damascus, people in and around the plains of Jericho, Caesarea, Nazareth, Corinth, Ephesus, Antioch, Phoenicia, Cyprus, the little villages nestled in the mountains of Lebanon, and even the isolated nomadic tribes of the deserts. All had an opportunity to accept or reject Jesus Christ! The last 1800 years of the Church, with all the combined efforts, have not produced the dramatic results of the first-century Church. They did it without mass communication techniques and without a quickly moving transportation system! "All they which dwelt in Asia heard the word of the Lord Jesus"! What a challenge! If they did it, we can do it in our day!

How did they do it? "Publicly, and from house to house"! They did it through a mobilization of all the Christians who spilled out of their cities into the towns, villages, and deserts—until all had heard! Christians went everywhere talking about Jesus Christ to everyone. They made every person conscious and aware of the message. Picture this scene happening in your town. You would see a spirit of expectancy everywhere! Whole cities could be reached! Churches would explode with growth! Christ would be honored and glorified! What an exciting description of evangelism, and it comes to us in simplicity as our pattern from that first Church.

To accomplish the task of worldwide evangelism, there must be a breaking down of many barriers. Perhaps the greatest breakthrough needed is new concepts, larger numbers, and a faith to believe it can happen. I personally believe we are on the very edge of seeing the greatest ingathering of souls into the Church this world has ever seen. Do you believe the Lord is going to take home a weak, small in number, failing Church? NO! The Church to be raptured out of the world is to be "the bride of Christ"—a vigorous, vital, vibrant, alive, overcoming, triumphant Bride—a Bride that is at her peak of condition!

The Challenge of World Evangelism Is ~~Here and Now~~ for this Generation

There will never be a better time than the present to be involved in evangelism! The future is now!

> Say not ye, There are yet four months, and then cometh the harvest? behold, I say unto you, Lift up your eyes, and look on the fields; for they are white already to harvest. And he that reapeth receiveth wages, and gathereth fruit unto life eternal: that both he that soweth and he that reapeth may rejoice together (John 4:35, 36).

If Christ gave this challenge to His followers nearly 2,000 years ago, how much more critical is it for today? The New Testament Church believed His directive and involved themselves in directly implementing the harvest!

To us, far too often, the challenge of the Great Commission has been viewed as a take-it-or-leave-it option. It is no option! It is not something we can do if we feel like it. *It is the message of the Church! It must be the first and foremost priority of the Church!* There will be no better day than today; no better opportunity than now. No greater message has ever been given; no greater hunger for the message has been seen than we are seeing now!

It can no longer be "church as usual" when you consider there are approximately 138,000 more lost people in the world today than there were yesterday! In 1 week, from Sunday to Sunday, there is over a 1-million increase! In the Assemblies of God, according to our own figures, the lost we won last year would have taken care of about 1 1/7 days' increase of the population growth! (The Update for 1979 showed us to have 163,780 conversions in our churches in America and 363,810 conversions in our overseas church. That's an exciting total—and one to be proud of!)

If we add our overseas conversions to our home conversions, the total is 527,590 for 1 year—that takes care of the increase of a bit less than 4 days! We are not even remotely keeping ahead of the increase, let alone going beyond the increase to reach the existing millions—4 billion today, but 6 billion by A.D. 2000!

Our task is laid out before us. It's not impossible or Christ would not have laid the burden on His church. Too often, in the past, we've looked at the vast size of the task and been overwhelmed by the immensity, so we have excused ourselves by saying, "It's too huge! The Lord can't be serious about holding me or my church responsible for world evangelism!"

Yes, He holds you and me and our churches responsible for the evangelization of this needy world! There is no way we can avoid it or get around this task. The only alternative open to us is to get on with the task!

He has promised resources we haven't even tapped! There are new methods, new techniques, exciting possibilities—but the message is still the same! His promise of direction and empowering is still the same: "And, lo, I am with you alway, even unto the end of the world. Amen" (Matthew 28:20).

Was the first-century Church obedient to the Great Commission? Yes! Note their response: "And they went forth, and preached everywhere, the Lord working with them, and confirming the word with signs following. Amen" (Mark 16:20).

The future is now for world evangelization! We are the

people of the harvest! Today is our day! Today is God's day of harvest!

Well, my friend, what are you waiting for? Let's get on with the harvest ... now!

Harvest conditions are upon us! The Church has been empowered! The Church has been directed! The Church is on a mission that cannot fail! The Holy Spirit has been given! The Lord Jesus Christ, King of kings and Lord of lords, has delayed His coming to allow for the harvest to be completed! Perhaps *you* will be the person to reap the very last soul into the kingdom of heaven before the final curtain shuts down on this life!

"*Blessed* are they that do his commandments, that they may have right to the tree of life, and may enter in through the gates into the city" (Revelation 22:14).

One more time .... what are you waiting for? The harvest is ready. The commandment has been given. YOU are the vital link in reaching the lost!

Let's all move into the harvest field ... TODAY!

We are on a mission like Jesus

Matthew 24:14 Says "and this Gospel of The Kingdom will be preached in the whole World as a Testimony to all Nations; Then the end will Come"

Bibliography

Allen, Charles L. and Mildred Parker. *How to Increase Your Sunday School Attendance*. Old Tappan, NJ: Fleming H. Revell Company, 1979.

Arn, Win, ed. *The Pastor's Church Growth Handbook*. Pasadena, CA: Church Growth Press, 1979.

Benjamin, Paul. *The Growing Congregation*. Lincoln, IL: Lincoln College Press, 1972.

Coleman, Robert E. *The Master Plan of Evangelism*. Old Tappan, NJ: Fleming H. Revell Company, 1971.

Eavey, C. B. *How to Be an Effective Sunday School Teacher*. Grand Rapids: Zondervan Publishing House, 1962.

Edwards, Gene. *How to Have a Soul Winning Church*. Springfield, MO: Gospel Publishing House, 1962.

Little, Paul E. *How to Give Away Your Faith*. Downers Grove, IL: InterVarsity Press, 1966.

McGavran, Donald A. and Winfield C. Arn. *Ten Steps for Church Growth*. San Francisco: Harper & Row, Publishers, 1977.

McIntyre, Ralph L. *Sunday School: Doorway to Church Growth*. Marion, IN: The Wesley Press, 1980.

Wagner, Peter C. *Your Spiritual Gifts Can Help Your Church Grow*. Glendale, CA: G/L Publications, 1980.